COORDINATED FED. TOOLS FROM WEST

COURTROOM HANDBOOK ON FEDERAL EVIDENCE
Steven Goode and Olin Guy Wellborn III

FEDERAL CIVIL RULES HANDBOOK
Steven Baicker-McKee, William Janssen, and John B. Corr

FEDERAL COURT OF APPEALS MANUAL
David G. Knibb

HANDBOOK OF FEDERAL EVIDENCE
Michael H. Graham

FEDERAL COURTS
Charles Alan Wright

FEDERAL JURY PRACTICE AND INSTRUCTIONS
Edward J. Devitt, Charles B. Blackmar, Michael A. Wolff, and Kevin O'Malley
[Also available in computer disk]

BENNETT'S GUIDE TO JURY SELECTION AND TRIAL DYNAMICS
Cathy S. Bennett and Richard B. Hirschhorn

BANKRUPTCY JURY MANAUL
Larry R. Ahern and Nancy Fraas MacLean

FEDERAL PRACTICE AND PROCEDURE
Charles Alan Wright, Arthur R. Miller, Mary Kay Kane, Edward H. Cooper, Richard L. Marcus, Kenneth W. Graham, and Victor James Gold
[Also available in CD-ROM]

WEST'S FEDERAL FORMS
A Group of Federal Practice Experts

LITIGATING CIVIL RIGHTS AND EMPLOYMENT DISCRIMINATION
Harold F. Lewis

CIRCUIT INSTRUCTIONS

Federal Judicial Center Pattern Criminal Jury Instructions
Fifth Circuit Pattern Jury Instructions (Civil Cases)
Fifth Circuit Pattern Jury Instructions (Criminal Cases)
Sixth Circuit Pattern Criminal Jury Instructions
Seventh Circuit Criminal Jury Instructions
Eighth Circuit Model Civil Jury Instructions
Eighth Circuit Model Criminal Jury Instructions

COORDINATED RESEARCH FROM WEST

Ninth Circuit Model Civil Jury Instructions
Ninth Circuit Model Criminal Jury Instructions
Eleventh Circuit Pattern Jury Instructions (Civil Cases)
Eleventh Circuit Pattern Jury Instructions (Criminal Cases)

WEST'S STATE JURY INSTRUCTIONS

Arkansas Model Jury Instructions—Civil
California Jury Instructions—Civil (BAJI) & Criminal (CALJIC)
Colorado Jury Instructions—Criminal
Illinois Pattern Jury Instructions—Civil & Criminal
Louisiana Jury Instructions—Civil & Criminal
Minnesota Jury Instructions—Civil & Criminal
Mississippi Model Jury Instructions—Civil & Criminal
Missouri Approved Jury Instructions—Civil
Nebraska Civil Jury Instructions
Tennessee Pattern Jury Instructions—Civil & Criminal
Virginia Jury Instructions
Washington Pattern Jury Instructions—Civil & Criminal

WESTLAW®

WEST*Check*® and WESTMATE®

West CD–ROM Libraries™

WEST*fax*®

WestDoc

West Books, CD–ROM Libraries, Disk Products, and WESTLAW
The Ultimate Research System

To order any of these West federal practice tools, call your West Representative or 1–800–328–9352.

NEED RESEARCH HELP?

If you have research questions concerning WESTLAW or West books, call West's Reference Attorneys at 1–800–733–2889.

PATTERN JURY INSTRUCTIONS

(Civil Cases)

Prepared by the
Committee on Pattern
Jury Instructions
District Judges Association
Fifth Circuit

1997 Edition

ST. PAUL, MINN.
WEST PUBLISHING CO.
1997

COMMITTEE ON PATTERN JURY INSTRUCTIONS DISTRICT JUDGES ASSOCIATION FIFTH CIRCUIT

Judge Martin L.C. Feldman, Chairman

Judge Edith Brown Clement

Judge Howell Cobb

Judge Rebecca Doherty

Judge Walter Gex

Judge Melinda Harmon

Judge Frank Polozola

Judge Mary Lou Robinson

Judge Sarah S. Vance

*

FOREWORD

This work contains general civil jury instructions and special instructions for the most frequently recurring federal question cases. These instructions are illustrative only. They attempt to present the applicable law in language that is precise, clear and brief. Judges are encouraged to modify the instructions or the order in which they are presented to the jury in any manner that will further these goals.

The instructions are not totally gender neutral. The committee elected not to adhere rigidly to a (he) (she) (it) format for several reasons. One is that in some types of cases, one gender predominates as a plaintiff or defendant. More importantly, however, it was felt that the rigid gender neutral format would make the instructions less readable and comprehensible to a jury. Thus in many instances the instructions must be modified to reflect the proper gender of a party.

These jury instructions were revised and edited by a committee composed of Judge Martin L.C. Feldman, Eastern District of Louisiana, Chairman, and Judges Edith Brown Clement, Eastern District of Louisiana, Howell Cobb, Eastern District of Texas, Rebecca F. Doherty, Western District of Louisiana, Walter J. Gex, III, Southern District of Mississippi, Melinda Harmon, Southern District of Texas, Frank J. Polozola, Middle District of Louisiana, Mary Lou Robinson, Northern District of Texas and Sarah S. Vance, Eastern District of Louisi-ana.

Professors Frank L. Maraist and Thomas C. Galligan of the Louisiana State University Law Center served as reporters to the Committee.

This project was funded by the Bar Association of the Fifth Federal Circuit.

*

WESTLAW® ELECTRONIC RESEARCH GUIDE

Coordinating Legal Research With WESTLAW

Pattern Jury Instructions is an essential aid to legal research. WESTLAW provides a vast, online library of over 8000 collections of documents and services that can supplement research begun in this publication, encompassing:

- Federal and state primary law (statutes, regulations, rules, and case law), including West's editorial enhancements, such as headnotes, Key Number classifications, annotations

- Secondary law resources (texts and treatises published by West Publishing Company and by other publishers, as well as law reviews)

- Legal news

- Directories of attorneys and experts

- Court records and filings

- Citators

Specialized topical subsets of these resources have been created for more than thirty areas of practice.

In addition to legal information, there are general news and reference databases and a broad array of specialized materials frequently useful in connection with legal matters, covering accounting, business, environment, ethics, finance, medicine, social and physical sciences.

This guide will focus on a few aspects of WESTLAW use to supplement research begun in this publication, and will direct you to additional sources of assistance.

Databases

A database is a collection of documents with some features in common. It may contain statutes, court decisions, administrative materials, commentaries, news or other information. Each database has a unique identifier, used in many WESTLAW commands to select a database of interest. For example, the database containing cases decided by the United States Courts of Appeal has the identifier CTA; the cases of a specific state are contained in a database having identifier XX-CS, where XX is the state's postal code.

The WESTLAW Directory is a comprehensive list of databases with information about each database, including the types of documents each contains. The first page of a standard or customized WESTLAW Directory is displayed upon signing on to WESTLAW, except when prior, saved research is resumed. To access the WESTLAW Directory at any time, enter DB.

Databases of potential interest in connection with your research include:

CTA5	5th Circuit Court of Appeals Cases
FED5-ALL 5th	Circuit Federal Cases
CTA5-ALL 5th	Circuit Federal and State Cases

For information as to currentness and search tips regarding any WESTLAW database, enter the SCOPE command SC followed by the database identifier (e.g., SC CTA). It is not necessary to include the identifier to obtain scope information about the currently selected database.

WESTLAW Highlights

Use of this publication may be supplemented through the WESTLAW Bulletins (WLB and WSB-XX) and various Topical Highlights, including Federal Practice and Procedure Highlights (WTH-FPP). Highlights databases contain summaries of significant judicial, legislative and administrative developments and are updated daily; they are searchable both from an automatic list of recent documents and using general WESTLAW search methods for documents accumulated over time. The full text of any judicial decision may be retrieved by entering FIND.

Consult the WESTLAW Directory (enter DB) for a complete, current listing of other highlights databases.

Retrieving Cases Citing These Instructions

To retrieve cases citing this publication, sign on to a case law database and enter a query, in the following form:

5 Fifth /7 Pattern /7 10.1

Retrieving a Specific Case

The FIND command can be used to quickly retrieve a case whose citation is known. For example:

FI 260 F.2d 790

WESTLAW ELECTRONIC RESEARCH GUIDE

Updating Case Law Research

There are a variety of citator services on WESTLAW for use in updating research.

Insta-Cite® may be used to verify citations, find parallel citations, ascertain the history of a case, and see whether it remains valid law. References are also provided to secondary sources, such as Corpus Juris Secundum®, that cite the case. To view the Insta-Cite history of a displayed case, simply enter the command IC. To view the Insta-Cite history of a selected case, enter a command in this form:

IC 831 F.2d 77

Shepard's® Citations provides a comprehensive list of cases and publications that have cited a particular case, with explanatory analysis to indicate how the citing cases have treated the case, e.g., "followed," "explained." To view the Shepard's Citations about a displayed case, enter the command SH. Add a case citation, if necessary, as in the prior Insta-Cite example.

For the latest citing references, not yet incorporated in Shepard's Citations, use Shepard's PreView® (SP command) and Quick-Cite™ (QC command), in the same way.

To see a complete list of publications covered by any of the citator services, enter its service abbreviation (IC, SH, SP or QC) followed by PUBS. To ascertain the scope of coverage for any of the services, enter the SCOPE command (SC) followed by the appropriate service abbreviation. For the complete list of commands available in a citator service, enter its service abbreviation (IC, SH, SP or QC) followed by CMDS.

Retrieving Statutes, Court Rules and Regulations

The United States Code and United States Code - Annotated are searchable databases on WESTLAW (identifiers USC and USCA, respectively), as are federal court rules (US-RULES) and regulations (CFR).

Annotated and/or unannotated versions of state statutes (XX-ST and XX-ST-ANN, respectively) and state court rules (XX-RULES) are also searchable on WESTLAW, as are the administrative codes of many states (XX-ADC).

In addition, the FIND command may be used to retrieve specific provisions by citation, obviating the need for database selection or search. To FIND a desired document, enter FI, followed by the citation of the desired document, using the full name of the publication, or one of the abbreviated styles recognized by WESTLAW.

If WESTLAW does not recognize the style you enter, you may enter one of the following, using US or any other state code in place of XX:

FI XX-ST	Displays templates for compiled statutes
FI XX-LEGIS	Displays templates for legislation
FI XX-RULES	Displays templates for rules
FI XX-ORDERS	Displays templates for court orders

Alternatively, entering FI followed by the publication's full name or an accepted abbreviation will normally display templates, useful jump possibilities, or helpful information necessary to complete the FIND process. For example:

FI USCA	Displays templates for United States Code - Annotated
FI FRAP	Displays templates for Federal Rules of Appellate Procedure
FI FRCP	Displays templates for Federal Rules of Civil Procedure
FI FRCRP	Displays templates for Federal Rules of Criminal Procedure
FI FRE	Displays templates for Federal Rules of Evidence
FI CFR	Displays templates for Code of Federal Regulations
FI FR	Displays templates for Federal Register

To view the complete list of FINDable documents and associated prescribed forms, enter FI PUBS.

Updating Research in re Statutes, Rules and Regulations

When viewing a statute, rule or regulation on WESTLAW after a search or FIND command, it is easy to update your research. A message will appear if relevant amendments, repeals or other new material are available through the UPDATE feature. Entering the UPDATE command will display such material.

Documents used to update federal statutes, rules, and regulations are searchable in the United States Public Laws (US-PL), Federal Orders (US-ORDERS) and Federal Register (FR) databases, respectively. For many states, similar material is contained in Legislative Service (XX-LEGIS), Court Orders (XX-ORDERS) and Administrative Register (XX-ADR) databases. Consult the WESTLAW Directory for availability in a specific state.

WESTLAW ELECTRONIC RESEARCH GUIDE

When documents citing a statute, rule or regulation are of interest, Shepard's Citations on WESTLAW may be of assistance. That service covers federal constitutional provisions, statutes and administrative provisions, and corresponding materials from many states. The command SH PUBS displays a directory of publications which may be Shepardized on WESTLAW. Consult the WESTLAW manual for more information about citator services.

Using WESTLAW as a Citator

For research beyond the coverage of any citator service, go directly to the databases (cases, for example) containing citing documents and use standard WESTLAW search techniques to retrieve documents citing specific constitutional provisions, statutes, standard jury instructions or other authorities.

Fortunately, the specific portion of a citation is often reasonably distinctive, such as 22:636.1, 301.65, 401(k), 12-21-5, 12052. When it is, a search on that specific portion alone may retrieve applicable documents without any substantial number of inapplicable ones (unless the number happens to be coincidentally popular in another context).

Similarly, if the citation involves more than one number, such as 42 U.S.C.A. § 1201, a search containing both numbers (e.g., 42 +5 1201) is likely to produce mostly desired information, even though the component numbers are common.

If necessary, the search may be limited in several ways:

A. Switch from a general database to one containing mostly cases within the subject area of the cite being researched;

B. Use a connector (&, /S, /P, etc.) to narrow the search to documents including terms which are highly likely to accompany the correct citation in the context of the issue being researched;

C. Include other citation information in the query. Because of the variety of citation formats used in documents, this option should be used primarily where other options prove insufficient. Below are illustrative queries for the U.S. Court of Appeals for the Fifth Circuit (CTA5) database:

Fed.R.Evid! F.R.Evid! F.R.E. Evidence Evid.! /7 401

will retrieve cases citing Federal Evidence Rule 401;

Fed.R.Civ! F.R.Civ! F.R.C.P. R.Civ! Civil Civ.! /7 16

WESTLAW ELECTRONIC RESEARCH GUIDE

will retrieve cases citing Federal Civil Procedure Rule 16; and

Fed.R.Ap! F.R.Ap! F.R.A.P. Appellate App.Proc! /8 22

will retrieve cases citing Federal Appellate Rule 22.

Alternative Retrieval Methods

WIN® (WESTLAW Is Natural™) allows you to frame your issue in plain English to retrieve documents:

When is motion for judgment on pleadings treated as summary judgment?

Alternatively, retrieval may be focused by use of the Terms and Connectors method:

HE(TREAT! /P JUDGMENT JUDGEMENT +3 PLEADINGS /P SUMMARY +1 JUDGMENT JUDGEMENT)

In databases with Key Numbers, either of the above examples will identify Federal Civil Procedure ⌐2533.1 as a Key Number collecting headnotes relevant to this issue if there are pertinent cases.

Since the Key Numbers are affixed to points of law by trained specialists based on conceptual understanding of the case, relevant cases that were not retrieved by either of the language-dependent methods will often be found at a Key Number.

Similarly, citations in retrieved documents (to cases, statutes, rules, etc.) may suggest additional, fruitful research using other WESTLAW databases (e.g., annotated statutes, rules) or services (e.g., citator services).

Key Number Search

Frequently, case law research rapidly converges on a few topics, headings and Key Numbers within West's Key Number System that are likely to contain relevant cases. These may be discovered from known, relevant reported cases from any jurisdiction; Library References in West publications; browsing in a digest; or browsing the Key Number System on WESTLAW using the JUMP feature or the KEY command.

Once discovered, topics, subheadings or Key Numbers are useful as search terms (in databases containing reported cases) alone or with other search terms, to focus the search within a narrow range of potentially relevant material.

WESTLAW ELECTRONIC RESEARCH GUIDE

For example, to retrieve cases with at least one headnote classified to Federal Civil Procedure ⇨2533.1, sign on to a caselaw database and enter

170Ak2533.1 [use with other search terms, if desired]

The topic name (Federal Civil Procedure) is replaced by its numerical equivalent (170A) and the ⇨ by the letter k. A list of topics and their numerical equivalents is in the WESTLAW Reference Manual and is displayed in WESTLAW when the KEY command is entered.

Other topics of special interest are listed below.

Abatement and Revival (2)
Action (13)
Arbitration (33)
Audita Querela (48)
Contribution (96)
Courts (106)
Damages (115)
Declaratory Judgment (118A)
Domicile (135)
Election of Remedies (143)
Estoppel (156)
Evidence (157)
Exceptions, Bill of (158)
Federal Courts (170B)

Habeas Corpus (197)
Injunction (212)
Interpleader (222)
Judges (227)
Judgment (228)
Jury (230)
Limitation of Actions (241)
Mandamus (250)
Prohibition (314)
Quo Warranto (319)
Removal of Cases (334)
Time (378)
United States Magistrates (394)
Witnesses (410)

Using JUMP

WESTLAW's JUMP feature allows you to move from one document to another or from one part of a document to another, then easily return to your original place, without losing your original result. Opportunities to move in this manner are marked in the text with a JUMP symbol (▶). Whenever you see the JUMP symbol, you may move to the place designated by the adjacent reference by using the Tab, arrow keys or mouse click to position the cursor on the JUMP symbol, then pressing Enter or clicking again with the mouse.

Within the text of a court opinion, JUMP arrows are adjacent to case cites and federal statute cites, and adjacent to parenthesized numbers marking discussions corresponding to headnotes.

On a screen containing the text of a headnote, the JUMP arrows allow movement to the corresponding discussion in the text of the opinion,

▶ (3)

WESTLAW ELECTRONIC RESEARCH GUIDE

and allow browsing West's Key Number System beginning at various heading levels:

- ▶ 170A   FEDERAL CIVIL PROCEDURE
- ▶ 170AXVII   Judgment
- ▶ 170AXVII(C)   Summary Judgment
- ▶ 170AXVII(C)3   Proceedings
- ▶ 170AK2533   Motion
- ▶ 170AK2533.1   k. In general.

To return from a JUMP, enter GB (except for JUMPs between a headnote and the corresponding discussion in opinion, for which there is a matching number in parenthesis in both headnote and opinion). Returns from successive JUMPs (e.g., from case to cited case to case cited by cited case) without intervening returns may be accomplished by repeated entry of GB or by using the MAP command.

General Information

The information provided above illustrates some of the ways WESTLAW can complement research using this publication. However, this brief overview illustrates only some of the power of WESTLAW. The full range of WESTLAW search techniques is available to support your research.

Please consult the WESTLAW Reference Manual for additional information or assistance or call West's Reference Attorneys at 1–800–REF–ATTY (1–800–733–2889).

For information about subscribing to WESTLAW, please call 1–800–328–0109.

TABLE OF CONTENTS

Instr.No.		Page
	1. PRELIMINARY INSTRUCTIONS	
1.1	Preliminary Instructions	1
	2. CAUTIONARY INSTRUCTIONS	
2.1	First Recess	5
2.2	Stipulated Testimony	6
2.3	Stipulations of Fact	7
2.4	Judicial Notice	8
2.5	Discontinuance as to Some Parties	9
2.6	Publicity During Trial	10
2.7	Bench Conferences and Recesses	11
2.8	Demonstrative Evidence	12
2.9	Witness Not Called	13
2.10	Similar Acts—Cautionary Charge	14
2.11	Duty to Deliberate	15
2.12	Instructions on Deliberation	16
2.13	Bias—Corporate Party Involved	17
2.14	Clear and Convincing Evidence	18
2.15	Limiting Instruction	19
2.16	Impeachment by Witnesses' Inconsistent Statements	20
2.17	Impeachment by Witnesses' Felony Conviction	21
2.18	Consideration of the Evidence	22
2.19	Expert Witnesses	23
2.20	Burden of Proof When Only Plaintiff Has Burden	24
2.21	Use of Notes Taken by Jurors	25
2.22	Cautionary Instruction on Damages	26
2.23	Deposition Testimony	27
	3. GENERAL INSTRUCTIONS FOR CHARGE	
3.1	General Instructions for Charge	29
	4. ADMIRALTY	
4.1	Seaman Status	33

TABLE OF CONTENTS

Instr.No.		Page
4.2	Vessels	37
4.3	Jones Act—Unseaworthiness—Maintenance and Cure—Loss of Society (Seaman Status Not Contested)	38
4.4	Jones Act—Negligence	39
4.5	Unseaworthiness	41
4.6	Causation	43
4.7	Contributory Negligence	44
4.8	Damages	46
4.9	Loss of Society	48
4.10	Punitive Damages	50
4.11	Maintenance and Cure (Appended to Jones Act—Unseaworthiness Claims)	51
4.12	Loss of Future Earnings (Replacement for Culver II)	55
4.13	Section 905(b) Longshore and Harbor Worker's Compensation Act Claim	56

5. RAILROAD EMPLOYEES

5.1	Federal Employers Liability Act (45 U.S.C. Section 51 et seq.)	63
5.2	Federal Safety Appliance Act (45 U.S.C. Section 1 et seq.)	66

6. ANTITRUST

6.1	Sherman Act (Section 1—Per Se Violation)	67
6.2	(Section 1—Per Se Violation)	73

7. SECURITIES ACT

7.1	Securities Act	79

8. RICO

8.1	RICO Claims	83

9. PATENT INFRINGEMENT

9.1	Patent Infringement	101

10. CIVIL RIGHTS

10.1	42 USC Section 1983 (Unlawful Arrest—Unlawful Search—Excessive Force) Qualified Immunity—Good Faith Defense	111

TABLE OF CONTENTS

Instr.No.		Page
10.2	Alternative Excessive Force Section 1983 Jury Charge	116
10.3	Civil Rights—42 USC Section 1983 (Superior Officers and Municipalities)	120
10.4	Civil Rights—42 USC Section 1983 (Adverse Employment Decision—Exercise of First Amendment Rights)	121
10.5	Eighth Amendment (Excessive Force)	125
10.6	Eighth Amendment (Inadequate Medical Care)	127
10.7	Eighth Amendment (Conditions of Confinement)	129

11. LABOR AND EMPLOYMENT CLAIMS

11.1	Fair Labor Standards Act (29 U.S.C. Sec. 216)	131
11.2	Age Discrimination in Employment Act (29 U.S.C. Sections 621–634)	134
11.3	Employee's Claim Against Employer and Union	136

12. TAX REFUNDS

12.1	Reasonable Compensation to Stockholder—Employee	139
12.2	Debt vs. Equity	142
12.3	Employee vs. Independent Contractor	147
12.4	Business Loss vs. Hobby Loss	150
12.5	Real Estate Held Primarily for Sale	152
12.6	Section 6672 Penalty	155
12.7	Gifts in Contemplation of Death	158

13. MISCELLANEOUS FEDERAL CLAIMS

13.1	Automobile Dealers Day–In–Court Act (15 U.S.C. Section 1221)	161
13.2	Odometer Requirements, Motor Vehicle Information and Cost Savings Act (15 U.S.C. Section 1981)	163
13.3	Eminent Domain	165
13.4	Interstate Land Sales Full Disclosure Act (15 U.S.C. Section 1709)	167

14. MISCELLANEOUS FEDERAL DEFENSES

14.1	Statute of Limitations Defense	169

15. DAMAGES

15.1	Consider Damages Only if Necessary	171
15.2	Compensatory Damages	172
15.3	Calculation of Past and Future Damages	174

TABLE OF CONTENTS

Instr.No.		Page
15.4	Injury/Pain/Disability/Disfigurement/Loss of Capacity for Enjoyment of Life	176
15.5	Aggravation or Activation of Disease or Defect	177
15.6	Medical Expenses	178
15.7	Lost Earnings/Time/Earning Capacity	179
15.8	Spouse's Loss of Consortium and Services	180
15.9	Parent's Loss of Child's Services, Earnings, Earning Capacity	181
15.10	Property Damage	182
15.11	Wrongful Death—Estate Damages	183
15.12	Wrongful Death—Survivors' Damages	184
15.13	Punitive Damages	186
15.14	Multiple Claims—Multiple Defendants	188
15.15	Mitigation of Damages	190

PATTERN JURY INSTRUCTIONS

(Civil Cases)

1. PRELIMINARY INSTRUCTIONS

WESTLAW Electronic Research
See WESTLAW Electronic Research Guide preceding the Table of Contents.

1.1

PRELIMINARY INSTRUCTIONS

MEMBERS OF THE JURY:

You have now been sworn as the jury to try this case. As the jury you will decide the disputed questions of fact.

As the Judge, I will decide all questions of law and procedure. From time to time during the trial and at the end of the trial, I will instruct you on the rules of law that you must follow in making your decision.

Soon, the lawyers for each of the parties will make what is called an opening statement. Opening statements are intended to assist you in understanding the evidence. What the lawyers say is not evidence.

After the opening statements, the plaintiff will call witnesses and present evidence. Then, the defendant will have an opportunity to call witnesses and present evidence. After the parties' main case is completed, the plaintiff may be permitted to present rebuttal evidence. After all the evidence is completed, the lawyers will again address you to make final arguments. Then I will instruct you on the applicable law. You will then retire to deliberate on a verdict.

Keep an open mind during the trial. Do not decide any fact until you have heard all of the evidence, the closing arguments, and my instructions.

Pay close attention to the testimony and evidence. [Do not take notes.]

[Alternate 1: You will need to rely on your memories.]

[Alternate 2: If you would like to take notes during the trial, you may do so. If you do take notes, be careful not to get so involved in note taking that you become distracted and miss part of the testimony. Your notes are to be used only as aids to your memory, and if your memory should later be different from your notes, you should rely on your memory and not on your notes. If you do not take notes, rely on your own independent memory of the testimony. Do not be unduly influenced by the notes of other jurors. A juror's notes are not entitled to any greater weight than the-recollection of each juror concerning the testimony.] Even though the court reporter is making stenographic notes of everything that is said, a typewritten copy of the testimony will not be available for your use during deliberations. On the other hand, any exhibits [may] [will] be available to you during your deliberations.

Until this trial is over, do not discuss this case with anyone and do not permit anyone to discuss this case in your presence. Do not discuss the case even with the other jurors until all of the jurors are in the jury room actually deliberating at the end of the case. If anyone should attempt to discuss this case or to approach you concerning the case, you should inform the Court immediately. Hold yourself completely apart from the people involved in the case—the parties, the witnesses, the attorneys and persons associated with them. It is im-

PRELIMINARY INSTRUCTIONS 1.1

portant not only that you be fair and impartial but that you also appear to be fair and impartial.

Do not make any independent investigation of any fact or matter in this case. You are to be guided solely by what you see and hear in this trial. Do not learn anything about the case from any other source. [In particular, do not read any newspaper account of this trial or listen to any radio or television newscast concerning it.] [Do not listen to any local radio or television newscasts until this trial is over, or read any local newspaper unless someone else first removes any possible reference to this trial.]

During the trial, it may be necessary for me to confer with the lawyers out of your hearing or to conduct a part of the trial out of your presence. I will handle these matters as briefly and as conveniently for you as I can, but you should remember that they are a necessary part of any trial.

It is now time for the opening statements.

*

2. CAUTIONARY INSTRUCTIONS

WESTLAW Electronic Research

See WESTLAW Electronic Research Guide preceding the Table of Contents.

2.1

FIRST RECESS

We are about to take our first break during the trial and I want to remind you of the instruction I gave you earlier. Until the trial is over, you are not to discuss this case with anyone, including your fellow jurors, members of your family, people involved in the trial, or anyone else. If anyone approaches you and tries to talk to you about the case, do not tell your fellow jurors but advise me about it immediately. Do not read or listen to any news reports of the trial. Finally, remember to keep an open mind until all the evidence has been received and you have heard the views of your fellow jurors.

If you need to speak with me about anything, simply give a signed note to the marshal to give to me.

I may not repeat these things to you before every break that we take, but keep them in mind throughout the trial.

2.2

STIPULATED TESTIMONY

The parties have agreed or stipulated that [e.g., if _____ were called as a witness he would testify that _____]. The agreement is that that would be [_____'s] testimony if called as a witness. You should consider that testimony in the same way as if it had been given here in court, and give it the value you believe it deserves.

2.3

STIPULATIONS OF FACT

The parties have agreed, or stipulated, that [_____]. This means that both sides agree that this is a fact. You must therefore treat this fact as having been proved.

2.4

JUDICIAL NOTICE

Although no evidence has been presented, I instruct you that you must accept as proved [state the facts].

2.5

DISCONTINUANCE AS TO SOME PARTIES

_____ and _____ are no longer involved in this trial. As jurors, it is your duty to consider the issues between [among] (identify remaining parties) under the instructions I give you after you have heard all of the evidence [which might still concern _____ and _____'s conduct in this dispute].

2.6

PUBLICITY DURING TRIAL

If there is publicity about this trial, you must ignore it. You must decide this case only from the evidence presented in the trial. Do not read anything or listen to any TV or radio programs about the case. [This instruction can be modified according to the extent of the case's notoriety].

2.7

BENCH CONFERENCES AND RECESSES

At times during the trial it may be necessary for me to talk with the lawyers here at the bench out of your hearing, or by calling a recess. We meet because often during a trial something comes up that doesn't involve the jury.

2.8

DEMONSTRATIVE EVIDENCE

Exhibit [describe] is an illustration. It is a party's [description or picture or model] to describe something involved in this trial. If your recollection of the evidence differs from the exhibit, rely on your recollection.

2.9

WITNESS NOT CALLED

(Name of Witness) _____ was available to both sides. Thus [the plaintiff] [the defendant] cannot complain that (Witness) was not called to testify, because (Party) could have called (Witness). [*This instruction is appropriate only if the issue arises during closing argument or at some other time in trial.*]

2.10

SIMILAR ACTS—CAUTIONARY CHARGE [1]

Evidence that an act was done at one time or on one occasion is not any evidence or proof whatever that the act was done in this case.

Then how may you consider evidence of similar acts?

You may consider evidence of similar acts for the limited purpose of showing _____'s [motive, opportunity, intent, knowledge, plan, identity, or absence of mistake or accident] which is at issue in this case.

Such evidence may not be considered for any other purpose whatsoever. You can't use it to reflect on _____'s character.

---

[1]. This is a charge pursuant to FRE 404B and should not be used if the evidence is otherwise admissible as circumstantial evidence of the act at issue in the case [prior or subsequent occurrence; see, e.g., McCormick on Evidence, Third Edition, Sec. 200, West Pub. Co., 1984; Hicks v. Six Flags Over Mid–America, 821 F.2d 1311 (8th Cir.1987) and the cases cited therein].

CAUTIONARY INSTRUCTIONS **2.11**

2.11

DUTY TO DELIBERATE

It is your sworn duty as jurors to discuss the case with one another in an effort to reach agreement if you can do so. Each of you must decide the case for yourself, but only after full consideration of the evidence with the other members of the jury. While you are discussing the case, do not hesitate to re-examine your own opinion and change your mind if you become convinced that you are wrong. However, do not give up your honest beliefs solely because the others think differently, or merely to finish the case.

Remember that in a very real way you are the judges—judges of the facts. Your only interest is to seek the truth from the evidence in the case.

2.12

INSTRUCTIONS ON DELIBERATION

When you retire to the jury room to deliberate, you may take with you [this charge and] the exhibits that the Court has admitted into evidence. Select your Foreperson and conduct your deliberations. If you recess during your deliberations, follow all of the instructions that I have given you concerning your conduct during the trial. After you have reached your unanimous verdict, your Foreperson must fill in your answers to the written questions and sign and date the verdict form. [Return this charge together with your written answers to the questions.] Unless I direct you otherwise, do not reveal your answers until such time as you are discharged. You must never disclose to anyone, not even to me, your numerical division on any question.

If you want to communicate with me at any time, please give a written message to the bailiff, who will bring it to me. I will then respond as promptly as possible either in writing or by meeting with you in the courtroom. I will always first show the attorneys your question and my response before I answer your question.

After you have reached a verdict, you are not required to talk with anyone about the case unless I order you to do so.

You may now retire to the jury room to conduct your deliberations.

2.13

BIAS—CORPORATE PARTY INVOLVED

Do not let bias, prejudice or sympathy play any part in your deliberations. A corporation and all other persons are equal before the law and must be treated as equals in a court of justice.

2.14

CLEAR AND CONVINCING EVIDENCE

Clear and convincing evidence is evidence that produces in your mind a firm belief or conviction as to the matter at issue. This involves a greater degree of persuasion than is necessary to meet the preponderance of the evidence standard; however, proof to an absolute certainty is not required.

2.15

LIMITING INSTRUCTION

You will recall that during the course of this trial I instructed you that I admitted certain testimony [and certain exhibits] for a limited purpose and I instructed you that you may consider some testimony [and documents] as evidence against one party but not against another. You may consider such evidence only for the specific limited purposes for which it was admitted. [Specific limiting instructions may be repeated as appropriate.]

2.16

IMPEACHMENT BY WITNESSES' INCONSISTENT STATEMENTS

In determining the weight to give to the testimony of a witness, you should ask yourself whether there was evidence tending to prove that the witness testified falsely about some important fact, or, whether there was evidence that at some other time the witness said [or did] something, [or failed to say or do something] that was different from the testimony he gave at the trial.[1]

---

[1] This charge may be elaborated on in the following manner:

You should remember that a simple mistake by a witness does not necessarily mean that the witness was not telling the truth. People may tend to forget some things or remember other things inaccurately. If a witness has made a misstatement, you must consider whether it was simply an innocent lapse of memory or an intentional falsehood, and that may depend upon whether it concerns an important fact or an unimportant detail.

2.17

IMPEACHMENT BY WITNESSES' FELONY CONVICTION

In weighing the credibility of a witness, you may consider the fact that he has previously been convicted of a felony [a crime involving dishonesty or false statement]. Such a conviction does not necessarily destroy the witness' credibility, but it is one of the circumstances you may take into account in determining the weight to give to his testimony.

2.18

CONSIDERATION OF THE EVIDENCE

You must consider only the evidence in this case. However, you may draw such reasonable inferences from the testimony and exhibits as you feel are justified in the light of common experience. You may make deductions and reach conclusions that reason and common sense lead you to make from the testimony and evidence.

The testimony of a single witness may be sufficient to prove any fact, even if a greater number of witnesses may have testified to the contrary, if after considering all the other evidence you believe that single witness.

There are two types of evidence you may consider. One is direct evidence—such as testimony of an eyewitness. The other is indirect or circumstantial evidence—the proof of circumstances that tend to prove or disprove the existence or nonexistence of certain other facts. The law makes no distinction between direct and circumstantial evidence, but simply requires that you find the facts from a preponderance of all the evidence, both direct and circumstantial.

2.19

EXPERT WITNESSES

When knowledge of technical subject matter may be helpful to the jury, a person who has special training or experience in that technical field—he is called an expert witness—is permitted to state his opinion on those technical matters. However, you are not required to accept that opinion. As with any other witness, it is up to you to decide whether to rely upon it.[1]

---

1. This charge may be elaborated on in the following manner:

In deciding whether to accept or rely upon the opinion of an expert witness, you may consider any bias of the witness, including any bias you may infer from evidence that the expert witness has been or will be paid for reviewing the case and testifying, or from evidence that he testifies regularly as an expert witness and his income from such testimony represents a significant portion of his income.

2.20

BURDEN OF PROOF WHEN ONLY PLAINTIFF HAS BURDEN

In this case, the plaintiff must prove every essential part of his claim by a preponderance of the evidence.

A preponderance of the evidence simply means evidence that persuades you that the plaintiff's claim is more likely true than not true.

In deciding whether any fact has been proven by a preponderance of the evidence, you may, unless otherwise instructed, consider the testimony of all witnesses, regardless of who may have called them, and all exhibits received in evidence, regardless of who may have produced them.

If the proof fails to establish any essential part of the plaintiff's claim by a preponderance of the evidence, you should find for the defendant as to that claim.

2.21

USE OF NOTES TAKEN BY JURORS

Any notes that you have taken during this trial are only aids to your memory. If your memory differs from your notes, you should rely on your memory and not on the notes. The notes are not evidence. If you have not taken notes, you should rely on your independent recollection of the evidence and should not be unduly influenced by the notes of other jurors. Notes are not entitled to any greater weight than the recollection or impression of each juror about the testimony.

2.22

CAUTIONARY INSTRUCTION ON DAMAGES

You should not interpret the fact that I have given instructions about the plaintiff's damages as an indication in any way that I believe that the plaintiff should, or should not, win this case.

2.23

DEPOSITION TESTIMONY

Certain testimony will now be presented to you through a deposition. A deposition is the sworn, recorded answers to questions asked a witness in advance of the trial. Under some circumstances, if a witness cannot be present to testify from the witness stand, that witness' testimony may be presented, under oath, in the form of a deposition. Some time before this trial, attorneys representing the parties in this case questioned this witness under oath. A court reporter was present and recorded the testimony. The questions and answers will be read (shown) to you today. This deposition testimony is entitled to the same consideration [and is to be judged by you as to credibility] [and weighed and otherwise considered by you insofar as possible in the same way] as if the witness had been present and had testified from the witness stand in court.

*

3. GENERAL INSTRUCTIONS FOR CHARGE

WESTLAW Electronic Research
See WESTLAW Electronic Research Guide preceding the Table of Contents.

3.1

GENERAL INSTRUCTIONS FOR CHARGE

MEMBERS OF THE JURY:

You have heard the evidence in this case. I will now instruct you on the law that you must apply. It is your duty to follow the law as I give it to you. On the other hand, you the jury are the judges of the facts. Do not consider any statement that I have made in the course of trial or make in these instructions as an indication that I have any opinion about the facts of this case.

[After I instruct you on the law, the attorneys will have an opportunity to make their closing arguments.] [You have heard the closing arguments of the attorneys.] Statements and arguments of the attorneys are not evidence and are not instructions on the law. They are intended only to assist the jury in understanding the evidence and the parties' contentions.

Answer each question from the facts as you find them. [Do not decide who you think should win and then answer the questions accordingly.] Your answers and your verdict must be unanimous.

You must answer all questions from a preponderance of the evidence. By this is meant the greater weight and degree of credible evidence before you. In other words, a preponderance of the evidence just means

3.1 PATTERN JURY INSTRUCTIONS

the amount of evidence that persuades you that a claim is more likely so than not so. In determining whether any fact has been proved by a preponderance of the evidence in the case, you may, unless otherwise instructed, consider the testimony of all witnesses, regardless of who may have called them, and all exhibits received in evidence, regardless of who may have produced them.

[You will recall that during the course of this trial I instructed you that certain testimony and certain exhibits were admitted into evidence for a limited purpose and I instructed you that you may consider some documents as evidence against one party but not against another. You may consider such evidence only for the specific limited purposes for which it was admitted. (Specific limiting instructions may be repeated as appropriate.)]

In determining the weight to give to the testimony of a witness, you should ask yourself whether there was evidence tending to prove that the witness testified falsely concerning some important fact, or whether there was evidence that at some other time the witness said or did something, or failed to say or do something, that was different from the testimony the witness gave before you during the trial.

You should keep in mind, of course, that a simple mistake by a witness does not necessarily mean that the witness was not telling the truth as he or she remembers it, because people may forget some things or remember other things inaccurately. So, if a witness has made a misstatement, you need to consider whether that misstatement was an intentional falsehood or simply an innocent lapse of memory; and the significance of that may depend on whether it has to do with an important fact or with only an unimportant detail.

[The fact that a witness has previously been convicted of a felony, or a crime involving dishonesty or false statement, is also a factor you may consider in weighing the credibility of that witness. Such a convic-

GENERAL INSTRUCTIONS FOR CHARGE 3.1

tion does not necessarily destroy the witness' credibility, but it is one of the circumstances you may take into account in determining the weight to give to his testimony.]

While you should consider only the evidence in this case, you are permitted to draw such reasonable inferences from the testimony and exhibits as you feel are justified in the light of common experience. In other words, you may make deductions and reach conclusions that reason and common sense lead you to draw from the facts that have been established by the testimony and evidence in the case.

The testimony of a single witness may be sufficient to prove any fact, even if a greater number of witnesses may have testified to the contrary, if after considering all the other evidence you believe that single witness.

There are two types of evidence that you may consider in properly finding the truth as to the facts in the case. One is direct evidence—such as testimony of an eyewitness. The other is indirect or circumstantial evidence—the proof of a chain of circumstances that indicates the existence or nonexistence of certain other facts. As a general rule, the law makes no distinction between direct and circumstantial evidence, but simply requires that you find the facts from a preponderance of all the evidence, both direct and circumstantial.

When knowledge of technical subject matter may be helpful to the jury, a person who has special training or experience in that technical field—he is called an expert witness—is permitted to state his opinion on those technical matters. However, you are not required to accept that opinion. As with any other witness, it is up to you to decide whether to rely upon it.

In deciding whether to accept or rely upon the opinion of an expert witness, you may consider any bias of the witness, including any bias you may infer from evidence that the expert witness has been or will be paid

3.1   PATTERN JURY INSTRUCTIONS

for reviewing the case and testifying, or from evidence that he testifies regularly as an expert witness and his income from such testimony represents a significant portion of his income.

[Any notes that you have taken during this trial are only aids to memory. If your memory should differ from your notes, then you should rely on your memory and not on the notes. The notes are not evidence. A juror who has not taken notes should rely on his or her independent recollection of the evidence and should not be unduly influenced by the notes of other jurors. Notes are not entitled to any greater weight than the recollection or impression of each juror about the testimony.]

When you retire to the jury room to deliberate on your verdict, you may take [this charge with you as well as] exhibits which the Court has admitted into evidence. Select your Foreperson and conduct your deliberations. If you recess during your deliberations, follow all of the instructions that the Court has given you about/on your conduct during the trial. After you have reached your unanimous verdict, your Foreperson is to fill in on the form your answers to the questions. Do not reveal your answers until such time as you are discharged, unless otherwise directed by me. You must never disclose to anyone, not even to me, your numerical division on any question.

If you want to communicate with me at any time, please give a written message or question to the bailiff, who will bring it to me. I will then respond as promptly as possible either in writing or by having you brought into the courtroom so that I can address you orally. I will always first disclose to the attorneys your question and my response before I answer your question.

After you have reached a verdict, you are not required to talk with anyone about the case unless the Court orders otherwise. [You may now retire to the jury room to conduct your deliberations.]

4. ADMIRALTY

WESTLAW Electronic Research
See WESTLAW Electronic Research Guide preceding the Table of Contents.

4.1

SEAMAN STATUS

The plaintiff is seeking damages from the defendant for injuries that he allegedly suffered as a result of an accident while he was performing (*describe task*).

The plaintiff's claim arises under the Jones Act. Only a seaman can bring a claim under the Jones Act. The plaintiff claims that his employment with the defendant was of such a nature that under the law he was a seaman and is entitled to bring this claim. The defendant denies that the plaintiff was a seaman and takes the position that the plaintiff is not entitled to bring this claim. You first must determine whether, at the time of the accident, the plaintiff was a seaman as the law defines that term. [*May be modified to reflect unseaworthiness claim.*]

As I instruct you about the test for seaman status, I also may use the term "member of a crew." Seaman and member of a crew mean the same thing.

The plaintiff is a seaman if he proves by a preponderance of the evidence that he performs the work of the vessel.[1] He performs the work of the vessel if and only if:

---

1. Where the claimant's connection is with a "fleet" of vessels, the term "fleet of vessels" should be substituted for the word "vessel." In addition, the jury should be charged in the following manner:

4.1   **PATTERN JURY INSTRUCTIONS**

    1. he was assigned permanently to a vessel or performed a substantial part of his work on a vessel; and

    2. the capacity in which he was employed or the duties that he performed contributed to the function of a vessel or to the accomplishment of the vessel's mission or to the operation or maintenance of the vessel during its movement or while at anchor for the vessel's future trips. A person need not aid in the navigation of a vessel in order to qualify as a seaman.

    The plaintiff must satisfy both the first and second parts of this test. If he satisfies both, then you must find that he was a seaman. In applying the first part of the test, you must determine whether, from a preponderance of the evidence, the plaintiff was either assigned permanently to the _____, the vessel, or whether he performed a substantial part of his work on it. The plaintiff need only to prove one of these to satisfy the first part of the test.

    Plaintiff was permanently assigned to the _____ if he had more than a temporary or occasional connection with the vessel, the _____. The plaintiff must prove that he had an actual regular connection with the _____.

    Even if you find that the plaintiff was not permanently assigned to the vessel as I have just defined it, he nevertheless can satisfy the first part of the test for seaman status if he performed a substantial part of his work on the vessel or if he performed a significant part of his work on the vessel with at least some degree of regularity and continuity and his duties on the vessel were more than merely fortuitous and incidental. (For example, a person who comes aboard to perform an isolated piece of work is not a seaman.) When a person

"A fleet of vessels is an identifiable group of vessels acting together or under one control." Barrett v. Chevron, U.S.A., Inc., 781 F.2d 1067 (5th Cir.1986).

ADMIRALTY **4.1**

performs some of his duties on land—[or in this case a platform]—and other of his duties on the vessel, you must consider the portion of his duties that he performed in each location in connection with your determination as to whether or not he performed a substantial or significant part of his work on the vessel, as compared to what he did on land [on the platform]. In other words, in determining whether or not the plaintiff was a seaman at the time of the accident, you must look at the nature and location of his work for the defendant taken as a whole. If the plaintiff's regularly assigned duties required him to divide his work time between vessel and land (or platform), you must determine his status as a seaman in the context of his entire employment with his employer, _____, not just his duties at the time he was injured.

(If plaintiff had a change in work assignment only.)

If, however, you find that the plaintiff's employment with _____ was changed before the accident, then you must determine whether the plaintiff was a seaman on the basis of his activities in his new assignment. Under the law, a person may change his employment with the same employer if his work duties or his work location are changed permanently.

If you find that the plaintiff was assigned permanently to the _____ or that he performed a substantial part of his work on the _____, you must then determine whether the plaintiff's duties were such that he meets the second part of the test. The plaintiff meets the second part of the test if he proves by a preponderance of the evidence that the job or duties he performed contributed to the function of the vessel, the _____, or to the accomplishment of its mission or to its operation or maintenance during its voyages or during its anchorage for its future trips. A person may contribute to the function of the vessel or the accomplishment of its

35

4.1 PATTERN JURY INSTRUCTIONS

mission although he is not engaged in actual navigation of the vessel.

Note

McDermott International, Inc. v. Wilander, 498 U.S. 337, 111 S.Ct. 807, 112 L.Ed.2d 866 (1991). See Southwest Marine, Inc. v. Byron Gizoni, 502 U.S. 81, 112 S.Ct. 486, 116 L.Ed.2d 405 (1991).

Barrett v. Chevron, U.S.A., Inc., 781 F.2d 1067 (5th Cir.1986).

Offshore Co. v. Robison, 266 F.2d 769 (5th Cir.1959).

4.2

VESSELS

You must determine whether the _____ (name, or describe structure) was a vessel. A vessel is a structure designed or used in navigation for the transportation of passengers, cargo, or equipment across navigable waters. In determining whether [the _____ (the structure)] is a vessel, you may but need not consider whether it had the following features:

(1) Navigational aids;

(2) A racked bow;

(3) Lifeboats or other lifesaving equipment;

(4) Bilge pumps;

(5) Crew quarters; or

(6) Coast Guard registration.

You may also consider the size of the [_____ (the structure)], its ability to float, the permanence of its attachment to the shore or the water bottom, and the fact of its movement, if any, across navigable waters. However, the fact that the (structure) had any one of these features is not conclusive. They are merely factors that you might wish to consider in determining whether the [_____ (structure)] was a vessel.[1]

1. See Southwest Marine, Inc. v. Byron Gizoni, 502 U.S. 81, 112 S.Ct. 486, 116 L.Ed.2d 405 (1991). The structures at issue, regarding vessel status, were movable work platforms used in a ship repair yard. The Supreme Court held that whether such structures were vessels was a material fact issue in the summary judgment context. The structures were moved about within the repair yard by tugboats. They had no power themselves, means of steering, navigation lights, navigation aids, or living facilities.

4.3

JONES ACT—UNSEAWORTHINESS—MAINTENANCE AND CURE—LOSS OF SOCIETY (SEAMAN STATUS NOT CONTESTED)

The plaintiff, _____ [a seaman], is asserting three separate claims against the defendant in this case.

The plaintiff's first claim, under a federal law known as the Jones Act, is that his employer, _____, was negligent, and that _____'s negligence was a cause of his injuries. The plaintiff's second claim is that unseaworthiness of a vessel caused his injury. The plaintiff's third claim is for Maintenance and Cure.

You must consider each of these claims separately. The plaintiff is not required to prove all of these claims. He may recover if he proves any one of them. However, he may only recover those damages or benefits that the law provides for the claims that he proves; he may not recover the same damages or benefits more than once.

The plaintiff _____ seeks damages for the loss of society with her husband, plaintiff _____.[1]

---

1. The spouse of an injured seaman probably cannot recover damages for loss of consortium, either under the Jones Act or for the unseaworthiness of the vessel. See Miles v. Apex Marine Corp., 498 U.S. 19, 111 S.Ct. 317, 112 L.Ed.2d 275 (1990); Anglada v. Tidewater, Inc., 752 F.Supp. 722 (E.D.La.1990). But see Rayborn v. Zapata Offshore Co., __ F.Supp. __, No. 90–0467, slip op. (W.D.La. May 2, 1991); Verdin v. L & M Bo–Truc Rental, Inc., 1991 WL 87930 (E.D.La.1991). The Fifth Circuit has resolved the conflict among the district courts and held that the spouse of an injured seaman cannot recover for loss of consortium. Murray v. Anthony J. Bertucci Constr. Co., Inc., 958 F.2d 127 (5th Cir.1992); Michel v. Total Transp., Inc., 957 F.2d 186 (5th Cir.1992).

4.4

JONES ACT—NEGLIGENCE

Under the Jones Act, the plaintiff _____ must prove that his employer was negligent. Negligence is the doing of an act that a reasonably prudent person would not do, or the failure to do something that a reasonably prudent person would do, under the same or similar circumstances. The occurrence of an accident, standing alone, does not mean anyone's negligence caused the accident.

In a Jones Act claim, the word "negligence" is given a liberal interpretation. It includes any breach of duty that an employer owes to his employees who are seamen, including the duty of providing for the safety of the crew.

Under the Jones Act, if the employer's negligent act or omission played any part, no matter how small, in actually causing the plaintiff's injury[1], then you must find that the employer is liable under the Jones Act.

Negligence under the Jones Act may consist of a failure to comply with a duty required by law. Employers of seamen have a duty to provide their employees

---

1. The Supreme Court, in Consolidated Rail Corporation v. Gottshall, 512 U.S. 532, 114 S.Ct. 2396, 129 L.Ed.2d 427 (1994), held that a railroad, as part of its duty to provide its employees with a safe place to work under FELA, has a duty to avoid subjecting its workers to negligently inflicted emotional injury. The Court ruled that "injury" as used in that statute may encompass both physical and emotional injury. The Court further announced that a worker within the zone of danger of physical impact will be able to recover for emotional injury caused by fear of physical injury to himself, but a worker outside the zone of danger will not. Because FELA standards have been carried into the Jones Act, this zone of danger standard applies to Jones Act claims as well as FELA claims. Therefore, in Jones Act cases in which plaintiff sues for purely emotional injury, without physical impact but within the zone of danger which causes a fear of physical impact, it is recommended by the Committee that the jury be instructed in a manner consistent herewith. Whether a reasonable person under the circumstances would have had a fear of physical impact is a question for the jury.

with a reasonably safe place to work. If you find that the plaintiff was injured because the defendant failed to furnish him with a reasonably safe place to work, and that the plaintiff's working conditions could have been made safe through the exercise of reasonable care, then you must find that the defendant was negligent.

The fact that the defendant conducted its operations in a manner similar to that of other companies is not conclusive as to whether the defendant was negligent or not.

You must determine if the operation in question was reasonably safe under the circumstances. The fact that a certain practice has been continued for a long period of time does not necessarily mean that it is reasonably safe under all circumstances. A long accepted practice may be an unsafe practice. However, a practice is not necessarily unsafe or unreasonable merely because it injures someone.

A seaman's employer is legally responsible for the negligence of one of his employees while that employee is acting within the course and scope of his job [employment].

If you find from a preponderance of the evidence that the defendant assigned the plaintiff to perform a task that the plaintiff was not adequately trained to perform, you must find that the defendant was negligent.

4.5

UNSEAWORTHINESS

The plaintiff seeks damages for personal injury that he claims was caused by the unseaworthiness of the defendant's vessel, the _____.

A shipowner owes to every member of the crew employed on its vessel the absolute duty to keep and maintain the ship, and all decks and passageways, appliances, gear, tools, parts and equipment of the vessel in a seaworthy condition at all times.

A seaworthy vessel is one that is reasonably fit for its intended use. The duty to provide a seaworthy vessel is absolute because the owner may not delegate that duty to anyone. Liability for an unseaworthy condition does not in any way depend upon negligence or fault or blame. If an owner does not provide a seaworthy vessel—a vessel that is reasonably fit for its intended use—no amount of care or prudence excuses the owner.

The duty to provide a seaworthy vessel includes a duty to supply an adequate and competent crew. A vessel may be unseaworthy even though it has a numerically adequate crew, if too few persons are assigned to a given task.

However, the owner of a vessel is not required to furnish an accident free ship. He need only furnish a vessel and its appurtenances that are reasonably fit for their intended use and a crew that is reasonably adequate for their assigned tasks.

The shipowner is not required to provide the best appliances and equipment, or the finest of crews, on his vessel. He is only required to provide gear that is reasonably proper and suitable for its intended use, and a crew that is reasonably adequate.

In summary, if you find that the owner of the vessel did not provide an adequate crew of sufficient manpower to perform the tasks required, or if you find that the vessel was in any manner unfit in accordance with the law as I have just explained it to you and that this was a proximate cause of the injury, a term I will explain to you, then you may find that the vessel was unseaworthy and the shipowner liable, without considering any negligence on the part of the defendant or any of its employees.

However, if you find that the owner had a capable crew and appliances and gear that were safe and suitable for their intended use, then the vessel was not unseaworthy and the defendant is not liable to the plaintiff on the claim of unseaworthiness.

4.6

CAUSATION

Not every injury [1] that follows an accident necessarily results from it. The accident must be the cause of the injury.

In determining causation, different rules apply to the Jones Act Claim and to the unseaworthiness claim.

Under the Jones Act, for both the employer's negligence and the plaintiff's contributory negligence,[2] an injury or damage is considered caused by an act, or failure to act, if the act or omission played any part, no matter how small, in bringing about or actually causing the injury or damage.

In an unseaworthiness claim, the plaintiff must show, not merely that the unseaworthy condition was a cause of the injury but that such condition was a proximate cause of it. This means that the plaintiff must show that the act or omission played a substantial part [was a substantial factor] in bringing about or actually causing his injury, and that the injury was either a direct result or a reasonably probable consequence of the act or omission.

1. See Consolidated Rail Corp. v. Gottshall, 512 U.S. 532, 114 S.Ct. 2396, 129 L.Ed.2d 427 (1994), regarding claims for purely emotional injuries within the zone of danger of physical impact. If a claim for purely emotional injuries is made, without physical impact but within the zone of danger which causes a fear of physical impact, then an instruction should be given consistent with *Gottshall*. See also Pattern Instruction 4.4.

2. Gautreaux v. Scurlock Marine, Inc., ___ F.3d ___ (5th Cir.1997) (en banc) 1997 WL 87755.

4.7

CONTRIBUTORY NEGLIGENCE

The defendant contends that the plaintiff was negligent, and that the plaintiff's negligence caused or contributed to causing his injury. This is the defense of contributory negligence. The defendant has the burden of proving that the plaintiff was contributorily negligent. If the plaintiff was guilty of contributory negligence that contributed to his injury, he nevertheless may recover. However, the amount of his recovery will be reduced by the extent of his contributory negligence.

A seaman is obligated under the Jones Act to act with ordinary prudence under the circumstances. The circumstances of a seaman's employment include not only his reliance on his employer to provide a safe work environment, but also his own experience, training and education. In other words, under the Jones Act a seaman has the duty to exercise that degree of care for his own safety that a reasonable seaman would exercise in like circumstances.[1]

If you find that the defendant was negligent (the vessel was unseaworthy), and that the (negligence) (unseaworthiness) was a proximate (legal) cause of the plaintiff's injury, but you also find that the accident was due partly to the contributory negligence of the plaintiff, then you must determine the percentage the plaintiff's contributory negligence contributed to the accident. You will provide this information by filling in the appropriate blanks in the special interrogatories. Do not make any reduction in the amount of damages that you award to the plaintiff. I will reduce the damages that

---

1. Gautreaux v. Scurlock Marine, Inc., ___ F.3d ___ (5th Cir.1997) (en banc) 1997 WL 87755.

you award by the percentage of contributory negligence that you assign to the plaintiff.

4.8

DAMAGES

If you find that the defendant is liable, you must award the amount you find by a preponderance of the evidence as full and just compensation for all of the plaintiff's damages. [*If there is no issue of punitive damages for the jury, continue with this instruction. If there is, however, then this instruction should be prefaced with: You also will be asked to determine if the Defendant is liable for punitive damages, and, if so, you will be asked to fix the amount of those damages. Because the method of determining punitive damages and compensatory damages differ, I will instruct you separately on punitive damages. The instructions I now give you apply only to your award, if any, of compensatory damages.*] Compensatory damages are not allowed as a punishment against a party. Such damages cannot be based on speculation, for it is only actual damages—what the law calls compensatory damages—that are recoverable. However, compensatory damages are not restricted to actual loss of time or money; they include both the mental and physical aspects of injury, tangible and intangible. They are an attempt to make the plaintiff whole, or to restore him to the position he would have been in if the accident had not happened.

You should consider the following elements of damages, to the extent you find that the plaintiff has established such damages by a preponderance of the evidence: physical pain and suffering including physical disability, impairment, and inconvenience, and the effect of the plaintiff's injuries and inconvenience on the normal pursuits and pleasures of life; mental anguish and feelings of economic insecurity caused by disability; income loss in the past; impairment of earning capacity or ability in the future, including impairment in the normal progress in the plaintiff's earning capacity due to his physical condition; postmedical expenses; the reasonable value, not exceeding actual cost to the plaintiff, of medical care that you find from the evidence will be reasonably certain to be required in the future as a proximate result of the injury in question.

Some of these damages, such as mental or physical pain and suffering, are intangible things about which no evidence of value is required. In awarding these damages, you are not determining value, but you should award an amount that will fairly compensate the plaintiff for his injuries.

Any award you make to the plaintiff is not subject to income tax; neither the state nor the federal government will tax it. Therefore, you should determine the amount that plaintiff is entitled to receive without considering the effect of taxes upon it.

4.9

LOSS OF SOCIETY

In addition to the damages that the plaintiff _____ demands, plaintiff _____ seeks damages for loss of society with her husband, _____, which she claims she has suffered as a result of his accident.

The spouse of an injured person may recover damages for loss of society if she proves by a preponderance of the evidence that she has suffered loss of society with her husband and that that loss of society was caused by injuries to her husband that are attributable to the fault of the defendant.[1]

Loss of society covers only the loss of love, affection, care, attention, comfort, protection and sexual relations the spouse has experienced. It does not include loss of support or loss of income that the spouse sustains. And it does not include grief or mental anguish.

Therefore, if you find by a preponderance of the evidence that plaintiff _____ suffered loss of society with her husband, _____ as a result of injuries caused by the fault of the defendant, you may award her damages for loss of society. If, on the other hand, you find from a preponderance of the evidence that plaintiff _____ did not sustain loss of society with her husband _____ as a result of injuries attributable to the fault of

---

1. The spouse of an injured seaman probably cannot recover damages for loss of consortium, either under the Jones Act or for the unseaworthiness of the vessel. See Miles v. Apex Marine Corp., 498 U.S. 19, 111 S.Ct. 317, 112 L.Ed.2d 275 (1990); Anglada v. Tidewater, Inc., 752 F.Supp. 722 (E.D.La.1990). But see Rayborn v. Zapata Offshore Co., __ F.Supp. __, No. 90–0467, slip op. (W.D.La. May 2, 1991); Verdin v. L & M Bo–Truc Rental, Inc., 1991 WL 87930 (E.D.La.1991). The Fifth Circuit has resolved the conflict among the district courts and held that the spouse of an injured seaman cannot recover for loss of consortium. Murray v. Anthony J. Bertucci Constr. Co., Inc., 958 F.2d 127 (5th Cir.1992); Michel v. Total Transp., Inc., 957 F.2d 186 (5th Cir.1992).

the defendant, then you may not award her damages for loss of society.

You may not award damages for any injury or condition from which the plaintiffs may have suffered, or may now be suffering, unless it has been proved by a preponderance of the evidence that the accident proximately or directly caused such injury or condition.

4.10

PUNITIVE DAMAGES

1. Under General Maritime Law

You may but are not required to award punitive damages against a defendant who has acted willfully and wantonly. The purpose of an award of punitive damages is to punish the defendant and to deter him and others from acting as he did.[1]

A person acts willfully or wantonly if he acts in reckless or callous disregard of, or with indifference to, the rights of the plaintiff. An actor is indifferent to the rights of another, regardless of the actor's state of mind, when he proceeds in disregard of a high and excessive degree of danger that is known to him or was apparent to a reasonable person in his position.[2]

2. Unseaworthiness

You may, but are not required to, award punitive damages if you find that the shipowner, _____, wantonly or willfully failed to provide the plaintiff with a seaworthy vessel, and that failure was a proximate cause of the plaintiff's injuries.

---

[1] On the general subject of punitive damages and the guidelines to be considered in fashioning jury charges, see Pacific Mutual Life Insurance Co. v. Haslip, 499 U.S. 1, 111 S.Ct. 1032, 113 L.Ed.2d 1 (1991).

[2] Prosser and Keeton on Torts, Fifth Edition, Sec. 34, p. 213, West Publishing Company, 1984.

ADMIRALTY **4.11**

4.11

MAINTENANCE AND CURE (APPENDED TO JONES ACT—UNSEAWORTHINESS CLAIMS)

The plaintiff's third claim is that, as a seaman, he is entitled to recover Maintenance and Cure. This claim is separate and independent from both the Jones Act and the unseaworthiness claims of the plaintiff. You must decide this claim separately from your determination of his Jones Act and unseaworthiness claims.

Maintenance and Cure is a seaman's remedy. [If you determine that plaintiff was a seaman, you then must determine if he is entitled to maintenance and cure.] [Plaintiff is a seaman; thus you must determine whether he is entitled to maintenance and cure.]

Maintenance and cure provides a seaman, who is disabled by injury or illness while in the service of the ship, medical care and treatment, and the means of maintaining himself, while recuperating.

A seaman is entitled to maintenance and cure even though he was not injured as a result of any negligence on the part of his employer or any unseaworthy condition of the vessel. To recover maintenance and cure, the plaintiff need only show that he suffered injury or illness while in the service of the vessel on which he was employed as a seaman, without willful misbehavior on his part. The injury or illness need not be work related, it need only occur while the seaman is in the service of the ship. And maintenance and cure may not be reduced because of any negligence on the part of the seaman.

The "cure" to which a seaman may be entitled includes the cost of medical attention, including the services of physicians and nurses as well as the cost of hospitalization, medicines and medical apparatus.

4.11 PATTERN JURY INSTRUCTIONS

However, the employer does not have a duty to provide cure for any period of time during which a seaman is hospitalized at the employer's expense.

Maintenance is the cost of food and lodging, and transportation to and from a medical facility. A seaman is not entitled to maintenance for that period of time that he is an inpatient in any hospital, because the cure provided by the employer through hospitalization includes the food and lodging of the seaman.

A seaman is entitled to receive maintenance and cure from the date he leaves the vessel until he reaches the point of what is called "maximum cure." Maximum cure is the point at which no further improvement in the seaman's medical condition is reasonably expected. Thus, if it appears that a seaman's condition is incurable, or that the treatment will only relieve pain but will not improve a seaman's physical condition, he has reached maximum cure. The obligation to provide maintenance and cure usually ends when qualified medical opinion is to the effect that maximum possible cure has been accomplished.

If you decide that the plaintiff is entitled to maintenance and cure, you must determine when the employer's obligation to pay maintenance began, and when it ends. One factor you may consider in determining when the period ends is the date when the seaman resumed his employment, if he did so. However, if the evidence supports a finding that economic necessity forced the seaman to return to work prior to reaching maximum cure, you may take that finding into consideration in determining when the period for maintenance and cure ends.

If you find that the plaintiff is entitled to an award of damages under either the Jones Act or unseaworthiness claims, and if you award him either lost wages or medical expenses, then you may not award him maintenance and cure for the same period of time. That is because the plaintiff may not recover twice for the same loss of wages or medical expenses. However, the plaintiff may also be entitled to an award of damages for failure to pay maintenance and cure when it was due.[1]

A shipowner who has received a claim for maintenance and cure is entitled to investigate the claim. However, if after investigating the claim, the shipowner unreasonably rejects the claim for maintenance and cure, he is liable for both the maintenance and cure payments he should have made, and any compensatory damages caused by his unreasonable failure to pay. Compensatory damages may include any aggravation of the plaintiff's condition because of the failure to provide maintenance and cure.

Thus, you may award compensatory damages because the shipowner failed to provide maintenance and cure if you find by a preponderance of the evidence that:

1. The plaintiff was entitled to maintenance and cure;
2. It was not provided;
3. The defendant acted unreasonably in failing to provide maintenance and cure; and
4. The failure to provide the maintenance and cure resulted in some injury to the plaintiff.[2]

---

1. The existence and extent of the double recovery problem will vary from case to case. Avoidance of double recovery will require careful screening of the evidence and a jury charge tailored in each case to fit the evidence presented.

For example, if the value of the food and/or lodging supplied to the seaman by the vessel owner is included in the wage base from which loss of earnings is calculated, then those items must not again be awarded as maintenance.

Likewise, if a jury awards loss of earnings from date of injury to some date which is subsequent to the end of the voyage, then those same earnings can't again be awarded as part of maintenance recovery pursuant to the ship owner's obligation to provide wages till the end of the voyage.

See Colburn v. Bunge Towing, Inc., et al., 883 F.2d 372 (5th Cir.1989).

2. Morales v. Garijak, Inc., 829 F.2d 1355 (5th Cir.1987).

4.11 PATTERN JURY INSTRUCTIONS

If you also find that the shipowner's failure to pay maintenance and cure was not only unreasonable, but was willful, that is, with the deliberate intent to do so, you may also award the plaintiff attorney's fees. However, you should not award attorney's fees unless the shipowner acted willfully in disregard of the seaman's claim for maintenance and cure. The plaintiff may not recover attorney's fees for the prosecution of the Jones Act or unseaworthiness claims. Thus, you may award only those attorney's fees plaintiff incurred in pursuing the maintenance and cure claim and only if you find that the shipowner acted willfully in failing to pay maintenance and cure.[3]

The plaintiff may not recover attorney's fees for the prosecution of the Jones Act or unseaworthiness claims. You may award attorney's fees only if you find that the shipowner acted arbitrarily or with callous disregard, in failing to pay maintenance and cure.

---

[3] Guevara v. Maritime Overseas Corp., 59 F.3d 1496 (5th Cir. 1995), held punitive damages are not awardable even for willful failure to pay maintenance and cure.

4.12

LOSS OF FUTURE EARNINGS (REPLACEMENT FOR CULVER II)[1]

If you find that the plaintiff is entitled to an award of damages for loss of future earnings, there are two particular factors you must consider. First, you should consider loss after income taxes; that is, you should determine the actual or net income that plaintiff has lost or will lose, taking into consideration that any past or future earnings would be subject to income taxes. You must award the plaintiff only his net earnings after tax. This is so because any award you may make here is not subject to income tax. The federal or state government will not tax any amount which you award on this basis.

Second, an amount to cover a future loss of earnings is more valuable to the plaintiff if he received the amount today than if he received the same amount in the future. Therefore, if you decide to award plaintiff an amount for lost future earnings, you must discount it to present value by considering what return would be realized on a relatively risk free investment.

1. See Monessen Southwestern Railway Co. v. Morgan, 486 U.S. 330, 108 S.Ct. 1837, 100 L.Ed.2d 349 (1988).

4.13 PATTERN JURY INSTRUCTIONS

4.13

SECTION 905(b) LONGSHORE AND HARBOR WORKER'S COMPENSATION ACT CLAIM

Introduction

Note: A maritime worker who is a seaman has the Jones Act remedy against his employer, and an unseaworthiness claim against the operator of the vessel as to which he is a seaman, whether the vessel operator is his employer or not. A maritime worker who is not a seaman may claim LHWCA benefits from his employer, and may bring a negligence action [33 U.S.C. Sec. 905(b)] against the operator of the vessel on which he is working (and, in some cases, against his employer, if his employer is operating the vessel). The standards for liability under the Jones Act and unseaworthiness differ from those for liability under Section 905(b). The United States Supreme Court has said that the categories of maritime worker—seaman and non-seaman—are mutually exclusive,[1] and the U.S. Fifth Circuit Court of Appeals has ruled that if a worker is covered by the LHWCA, he cannot qualify for seaman status.[2] The U.S. Ninth Circuit Court of Appeals has reached the opposite conclusion, holding that the initial inquiry is whether the worker is a seaman, and the U.S. Supreme Court granted writs in the Ninth Circuit case. The Supreme Court affirmed the Ninth Circuit and, in doing so, impliedly overruled the Fifth Circuit ruling, which is now of doubtful value. Seaman status and LHWCA status are mutually exclusive, requiring independent determinations, as the facts of the case may require. A maritime worker is limited to LHWCA remedies only if

1. McDermott International, Inc. v. Wilander, 498 U.S. 337, 111 S.Ct. 807, 112 L.Ed.2d 866 (1991).
2. Pizzitolo v. Electro–Coal Transfer Corp., 812 F.2d 977 (5th Cir.1987).

no genuine issue of fact exists as to whether the worker was a seaman under the Jones Act.[3]

LHWCA STATUS

A worker is covered by the LHWCA if he is engaged in maritime employment and is injured at a place within the coverage of the act. These are two separate requirements.

A worker is engaged in maritime employment if:

(1) he is injured on actual navigable waters in the course of his employment on those waters,[4] or

(2) he is injured while engaged in an essential part of the loading or unloading process of a vessel.[5]

> Note: A special charge may be appropriate if reasonable minds could conclude that the plaintiff was engaged in the activities described in 33 USC Sec. 902(3)(A)–(H).[6]

A place is within the coverage of the act if it is either actual navigable waters, an area adjoining actual navigable waters, or an area adjoining an area adjoining actual navigable waters and customarily used by an employer in loading, unloading, building or repairing of a vessel.[7]

---

3. Southwest Marine, Inc. v. Byron Gizoni, 502 U.S. 81, 112 S.Ct. 486, 116 L.Ed.2d 405 (1991); See Gizoni v. Southwest Marine, Inc., 909 F.2d 385 (9th Cir.1990).

4. Director v. Perini North River Associates, 459 U.S. 297, 103 S.Ct. 634, 74 L.Ed.2d 465 (1983).

5. Chesapeake and Ohio Ry. Co. v. Schwalb, 493 U.S. 40, 110 S.Ct. 381, 107 L.Ed.2d 278 (1989), and cases cited therein.

6. These subsections exclude from the definition of maritime workers certain clerical, recreational, marina and aquaculture workers, employees of suppliers or vendors, suppliers or transporters temporarily doing business on a covered premise and not engaged in work normally performed by the employer, masters or members of the crew of a vessel, and certain persons employed to build, load, unload or repair certain vessels.

7. 33 U.S.C. § 903.

4.13 PATTERN JURY INSTRUCTIONS

Note: A special charge may be appropriate if reasonable minds could conclude that the plaintiff's employment fit within 33 USC Sec. 903(d).[8]

SECTION 905(b) NEGLIGENCE CHARGE

If you find that the plaintiff, _____, was covered by the LHWCA at the time of his injury, then you must determine whether plaintiff's injury was caused by the negligence of the defendant, the operator of the vessel _____. The defendant does not owe plaintiff the duty to provide a seaworthy vessel; the defendant is liable only if he was guilty of negligence which was the legal cause of the plaintiff's injury.

Negligence is the failure to exercise reasonable care under the circumstances. A vessel operator such as defendant must exercise reasonable care before the plaintiff's employer, a (here, insert "stevedore," or the other type of maritime employment in which the plaintiff's employer was engaged on the vessel) began its operations on the vessel. This means that the defendant must use reasonable care to have the vessel and its equipment in such condition that an expert and experienced (here, insert "stevedore," or the other type of maritime employment in which the plaintiff's employer was engaged on the vessel) would be able, by the exercise of reasonable care, to carry on its work on the vessel with reasonable safety to persons and property. This means that the defendant must warn the plaintiff's employer of a hazard on the ship, or a hazard with respect to the ship's equipment, if:

8. The cited section excludes from coverage certain employees injured while working in certain areas of a facility engaged exclusively in building, repairing or dismantling certain small vessels, unless the facility receives Federal maritime subsidies or the employee is not covered by a state worker compensation law.

The defendant knew about the hazard, or should have discovered it in the exercise of reasonable care, and

The hazard was one which was likely to be encountered by the plaintiff's employer in the course of his operations in connection with the defendant's vessel, and

The hazard was one which the plaintiff's employer did not know about, and which would not be obvious to or anticipated by a reasonably competent (stevedore, or other designated maritime employer) in the performance of his work. Even if the hazard was one about which the plaintiff's employer knew, or which would be obvious or anticipated by a reasonably competent (here, insert "stevedore" or the other type of maritime employment in which the plaintiff's employer was engaged on the vessel), the defendant must exercise reasonable care to avoid the harm to plaintiff if the hazard was one which defendant knew or should have known the plaintiff's employer would not or could not correct and the plaintiff could not or would not avoid.[9]

9. This sentence does not appear in the Scindia decision (see footnote 10, post) but appears warranted from a number of subsequent lower court decisions. See, e.g., Pluyer v. Mitsui O.S.K. Lines, Ltd., 664 F.2d 1243 (5th Cir.1982); Griffith v. Wheeling–Pittsburgh Steel Corp., 657 F.2d 25 (3d Cir.1981); Harris v. Reederei, 657 F.2d 53 (4th Cir.1981); Moore v. M.P. Howlett, Inc., 704 F.2d 39 (2d Cir.1983). The language selected should not conflict with the rule that the shipowner has no duty to anticipate the negligence of the stevedore. See, e.g., Polizzi v. M/V Zephyros II Monrovia, 860 F.2d 147 (5th Cir.1988). The Supreme Court has held, for example, that the exercise of reasonable care does not require the ship-owner to supervise the ongoing operations of the loading stevedore (or other stevedores who handle the cargo before its arrival in port) or to inspect the completed stow. Howlett v. Birkdale Shipping Co., S.A., 512 U.S. 92, 114 S.Ct. 2057, 129 L.Ed.2d 78 (1994), on remand, 1995 WL 27104 (E.D.Pa. 1995). In *Howlett*, the Supreme Court dealt with the turnover duty to warn of latent defects in the cargo stow and cargo area, and held that the duty is a narrow one.

4.13 PATTERN JURY INSTRUCTIONS

The standard of care which a vessel operator owes to the plaintiff after the plaintiff's employer began its operations on the vessel is different.

If, after the plaintiff's employer began operations on the vessel, the defendant actively involved itself in those operations, it is liable if it failed to exercise reasonable care in doing so, and such failure was the cause of plaintiff's injuries.

If, after the plaintiff's employer began operations on the vessel, the defendant maintained control over equipment or over an area of the vessel on which the plaintiff could reasonably have been expected to go in the performance of his duties, the defendant must use reasonable care to avoid exposing the plaintiff to harm from the hazards the plaintiff reasonably could have been expected to encounter from such equipment or in such area.

If, after the plaintiff's employer began its operations on the vessel, the defendant learned that an apparently dangerous condition existed (including a condition which existed before the plaintiff's employer began its operations) or has developed in the course of those operations, the defendant vessel owner must use reasonable care to intervene to protect the plaintiff against injury from that condition only if the plaintiff's employer's judgment in continuing to work in the face of such a condition was so obviously improvident that the defendant should have known that the condition created an unreasonable risk of harm to the plaintiff. In determining whether the plaintiff's employer's judgment is "so obviously improvident" that the defendant should have intervened, you may consider that the plaintiff's employer has the primary duty to provide a safe place to work for plaintiff and its other employees, and that the defendant ordinarily must justifiably rely upon the plaintiff's employer to provide his employees with a reasonably safe place to work. In determining whether the defendant justifiably relied upon the decision of the plaintiff's employer to continue the work despite the condition, you should consider the expertise of the plaintiff's employer, the expertise of the defendant, and any other factors which would tend to establish whether the defendant was negligent in failing to intervene into the operations of the plaintiff's employer.[10]

10. Scindia Steam Navigation Co. v. De Los Santos, 451 U.S. 156, 101 S.Ct. 1614, 68 L.Ed.2d 1 (1981); Randolph et al. v. Laeisz, 896 F.2d 964 (5th Cir.1990).

*

5. RAILROAD EMPLOYEES

WESTLAW Electronic Research

See WESTLAW Electronic Research Guide preceding the Table of Contents.

5.1

FEDERAL EMPLOYERS LIABILITY ACT (45 U.S.C. SECTION 51 ET SEQ.)

The plaintiff is making a claim under the Federal Employers Liability Act. To win, the plaintiff must prove each of the following elements by a preponderance of the evidence:

1. That at the time of the plaintiff's injury[1], he (she) was an employee of the defendant performing duties in the course of his (her) employment;

2. That the defendant was at such time a common carrier by railroad, engaged in interstate commerce;

3. That the defendant was "negligent"; and

---

1. The Supreme Court, in Consolidated Rail Corporation v. Gottshall, 512 U.S. 532, 114 S.Ct. 2396, 129 L.Ed.2d 427 (1994), held that a railroad, as part of its duty to provide its employees with a safe place to work under FELA, has a duty to avoid subjecting its workers to negligently inflicted emotional injury. The Court ruled that "injury" as used in that statute may encompass both physical and emotional injury. The Court further announced that a worker within the zone of danger of physical impact will be able to recover for emotional injury caused by fear of physical injury to himself, but a worker outside the zone of danger will not. Therefore, in cases in which plaintiff sues for purely emotional injury, without physical impact but within the zone of danger which causes a fear of physical impact, it is recommended by the Committee that the jury be instructed in a manner consistent herewith. Whether a reasonable person under the circumstances would have had a fear of physical impact is a question for the jury.

5.1 PATTERN JURY INSTRUCTIONS

4. That defendant's negligence was a "legal cause" of damage sustained by the plaintiff.

The plaintiff claims that the defendant was negligent because [*describe the specific act(s) or omission(s) asserted as negligence on the part of the defendant*].

Negligence is the failure to use reasonable care. Reasonable care is that degree of care that a reasonably careful person would use under like circumstances. Negligence may consist either in doing something that a reasonably careful person would not do under like circumstances, or in failing to do something that a reasonably careful person would do under like circumstances.

Negligence is a legal cause of damage if it played any part, no matter how small, in bringing about or actually causing the injury or damage. If you find that the defendant was negligent and that the defendant's negligence contributed in any way toward any injury or damage suffered by the plaintiff, you must find that such injury or damage was legally caused by the defendant's act or omission. Negligence may be a legal cause of damage even though it operates in combination with the act of another, or some natural cause, or some other cause, if the negligence played any part, no matter how small, in causing the damage.

If the plaintiff does not establish his claim by a preponderance of the evidence, your verdict must be for the defendant. If, however, plaintiff does establish his claim by a preponderance of the evidence, then you must consider the defense raised by the defendant.

The defendant contends that the plaintiff was negligent and that such negligence was a legal cause of the plaintiff's injury. The defendant bears the burden of proving that the plaintiff was negligent. The defendant must establish:

1. That the plaintiff was also negligent; and

RAILROAD EMPLOYEES 5.1

2. That such negligence was a legal cause of the plaintiff's own damage.

If you find that the defendant was negligent and that the plaintiff was negligent, then the plaintiff will not be barred from recovery, but his recovery will be reduced. Let me give you an example: If you find that the accident was due partly to the fault of the plaintiff, that the plaintiff's own negligence was, for example, 10% responsible for the damage, then you must fill in that percentage as your finding on the special verdict form that I will explain to you. Your finding that the plaintiff was negligent does not prevent him from recovering; I will merely reduce the plaintiff's total damages by the percentage that you insert. Of course, by using the number 10% as an example, I do not mean to suggest any specific figure to you. If you find that the plaintiff was negligent, you might find any amount between 1% and 99%.

5.2

FEDERAL SAFETY APPLIANCE ACT
(45 U.S.C. SECTION 1 ET SEQ.)

The plaintiff's claim is based upon the Federal Safety Appliance Act. Specifically, plaintiff claims that [*describe the specific act(s) or omission(s) asserted as a violation of the Act by the defendant*].

The relevant provision of the Federal Safety Appliances Act is:

[*Quote the relevant provision of the Act, 45 U.S.C. § 1 et seq.*]

If you find from a preponderance of the evidence that the defendant violated this provision of the Federal Safety Appliance Act and that the violation played any part, no matter how small, in bringing about or actually causing injury to the plaintiff, then the plaintiff is entitled to recover from the defendant such damages you determine the plaintiff actually sustained as a result of the violation. The defendant is liable for the damages caused by the violation, although the defendant was not negligent.

The negligence of the plaintiff is not a defense and does not reduce the recovery by the plaintiff for any damages caused by any violation of the Federal Safety Appliance Act.

[*Enumerate recoverable elements of damage with explanation, as appropriate, of the terms used in describing each element.*]

6. ANTITRUST

WESTLAW Electronic Research
See WESTLAW Electronic Research Guide preceding the Table of Contents.

6.1

SHERMAN ACT (SECTION 1—PER SE VIOLATION)

CONSPIRACY TO FIX PRICES
(INCLUDES ALTERNATIVE "RULE OF REASON" INSTRUCTION)

The plaintiff claims that the defendant violated the anti-trust laws.

[The purposes of the anti-trust laws are to preserve and advance the system of free and open competition, and to secure to everyone an equal opportunity to engage in business, trade, and commerce. This policy is the primary feature of the private free enterprise system. The law promotes the concept that free competition produces the best allocation of economic resources. However, it recognizes that in the natural operation of the economic system, some competitors are going to lose business while others prosper. An act becomes unlawful only when it constitutes an unreasonable restraint on interstate commerce.]

To establish his claim the plaintiff must prove the following elements by a preponderance of the evidence:

1. That there was a combination or conspiracy between the defendants to fix the price of _____;

2. That the combination or conspiracy constituted an unreasonable restraint on interstate commerce as I will define it;

3. That the restraint involved a substantial amount of such commerce; and
4. That the plaintiff suffered injury in his business or property as a proximate result of the alleged combination or conspiracy.

A combination or conspiracy is formed when two or more persons knowingly join together to accomplish some unlawful purpose by joint action. A person acts knowingly if he acts voluntarily and intentionally, and not by mistake or accident. The essence of a conspiracy is an agreement between two or more persons to violate or disregard the law. This does not mean that the members of an alleged conspiracy must enter into any [express or] formal agreement. The required combination or conspiracy may be established by showing that the defendant(s) knowingly came to a common and mutual understanding to accomplish or attempt to accomplish an unlawful purpose. A conspiracy cannot be formed unless at least two separate persons or corporations reach an agreement or understanding. A single corporation cannot agree, combine or conspire with its own officers or employees.

[However, one corporation can combine or conspire with another corporation if the two operate as separate entities. Affiliated parent-subsidiary corporations do not lose their separate existences merely because they are affiliated. On the other hand, no combination or conspiracy is possible between corporations that are commonly owned and controlled and that regularly conduct their business affairs in such a manner that they constitute, in effect, a single business entity. You must determine whether the defendants constituted separate and distinct corporate entities or a single, integrated business enterprise.]

Mere similarity of conduct among various persons, and the fact that they may have associated with each other, and may have assembled together and discussed common aims and interests, do not necessarily establish proof of the existence of a conspiracy. Likewise, a mere similarity of competitive business practices of the defendant(s) and others, or the fact that they may have charged identical prices for the same goods and services, do not necessarily establish a conspiracy because such practices may be consistent with ordinary competitive behavior in a free and open market.

As to the second element, the plaintiff must prove that the alleged conspiracy resulted in an unreasonable restraint on interstate commerce. A conspiracy to fix prices in interstate trade or commerce is, in and of itself, an unreasonable restraint of trade. It is immaterial whether the prices agreed to be fixed were reasonable or unreasonable. A price fixing conspiracy may consist of any agreement or arrangement or understanding between two or more competitors, knowingly made, to sell at a uniform price, or to raise, lower or stabilize prices. There is a price fixing conspiracy and an unreasonable restraint on interstate commerce in violation of the anti-trust laws if (1) there is a common plan or understanding, (2) knowingly made, or arranged, or entered into, (3) between two or more competitors, (4) who are engaged in interstate trade or commerce, (5) to adopt or follow or adhere to any price formula that results in raising, or lowering, or maintaining at fixed levels prices charged for goods or services sold in interstate trade or commerce.

(Alternative "Rule of Reason" Instruction)

[I have instructed you on price fixing and have instructed you that price fixing is unreasonable in and of itself. However, there is an exception to this rule. If you find that this case involves an industry in which restraints on competition are essential if the industry's product (or service) is to be available at all, or, if you find that this case does not involve a price fixing agreement, then the question of whether the alleged conspira-

6.1   PATTERN JURY INSTRUCTIONS

cy constituted an unreasonable restraint on interstate commerce must then be determined on the basis of full consideration of all of the facts and circumstances disclosed by the evidence, including the nature of the particular industry or the product or service involved, the market area involved, any facts that you find to be peculiar to that industry, product, service, or market area, the nature of the alleged restraint and its effect, actual or probable, and the history of the circumstances surrounding the alleged restraint and the reasons for adopting the particular practice that is alleged to constitute the restraint. In sum, the reasonableness of a restraint is judged by its general effect on the market, not by the circumstances of a particular application. An individual business decision that is negligent or based on insufficient facts or illogical conclusions is not a basis for antitrust liability.]

The third element requires the plaintiff to prove as a part of its claim that the alleged combination or conspiracy constituted a restraint on interstate commerce involving a substantial amount of such commerce. The term "interstate commerce" refers to business transacted across State lines or between persons having their residences or businesses in different States. It differs from intrastate commerce, which is business done within a single State. There can be no violation of the antitrust law unless you find that the challenged activities of the defendants have actually occurred in interstate commerce or, if only done within one State, that such activity constituted a restraint on interstate commerce involving a not insubstantial amount of such commerce. The plaintiff is not required to show that the disputed transactions were interstate transactions in and of themselves, if the plaintiff shows that such transactions have affected interstate commerce in a substantial way.

The fourth element that the plaintiff must establish as a part of its claim is that it suffered injury in its

ANTITRUST 6.1

business or property as a proximate result of the alleged combination or conspiracy. In the course of normal, lawful competition, some businesses may suffer economic losses or even go out of business. The anti-trust laws are violated only when unlawful competitive practices cause such economic losses. An injury to a business is the "proximate result" of an anti-trust violation only when the act or transaction constituting the violation directly and in natural and continuous sequence produces, or contributes substantially to producing, the injury. In other words, the defendant's alleged violation of the anti-trust laws must be a direct, substantial and identifiable cause of the injury that plaintiff claims to have suffered. Proof of an antitrust violation does not necessarily mean the plaintiff was damaged. Proof of an antitrust violation and antitrust injury must be shown independently. A plaintiff can recover only if the loss stems from a reduction in competition because of the defendant's(s') behavior. There is no antitrust injury unless that behavior reduced competition, even if the behavior violated the antitrust law at issue.[1]

In considering the evidence as to the conspiracy charged, you must first determine whether or not the conspiracy existed. If you conclude that the conspiracy did exist, you should next determine whether or not the

---

1. A private plaintiff bringing an action under the antitrust laws must show an "antitrust injury," i.e., he must show not only that he was injured by the defendant's anticompetitive conduct, but must also show that his injury was caused "by reason of" that which made the conduct anticompetitive. In Atlantic Richfield Co. v. USA Petroleum Co., 495 U.S. 328, 110 S.Ct. 1884, 109 L.Ed.2d 333 (1990), defendant engaged in an allegedly illegal vertical price fixing scheme that fixed maximum prices. The Court rejected plaintiff's claim because there was no "antitrust injury," i.e., injury to competition. "When prices are not predatory, any losses flowing from them cannot be said to stem from an anticompetitive aspect of the defendant's conduct." (495 U.S. at 340, 110 S.Ct. at 1892). See also, Brunswick Corp. v. Pueblo Bowl–O–Mat, Inc., 429 U.S. 477, 97 S.Ct. 690, 50 L.Ed.2d 701 (1977), and the cases cited in Atlantic Richfield Co. v. USA Petroleum Co., supra.

6.1 PATTERN JURY INSTRUCTIONS

defendant(s) was (were) a knowing member of the conspiracy.

If it appears from a preponderance of the evidence that the conspiracy was knowingly formed, and that the defendant(s) knowingly became a member of the conspiracy, then the plaintiff is entitled to the verdict. The ultimate success or failure of the conspiracy is immaterial, if the plaintiff sustained some damage as a result of the conspiracy.

If you find that the plaintiff is entitled to a verdict, the law provides that the plaintiff is to be fairly compensated for all damage, if any, to his business and property, that was proximately caused by the defendant's violation of the antitrust laws. In arriving at the amount of the award, you should include any damages the plaintiff suffered because of any profits he lost as a proximate result of the violation by the defendant(s) of the antitrust laws.

If you should find from a preponderance of the evidence that the defendant's illegal conduct proximately caused damage to the plaintiff's business and property, such as a loss of profits, then the fact that the precise amount of the plaintiff's damages may be difficult to ascertain should not affect the plaintiff's recovery.

However, you may not award the plaintiff purely speculative damages. You may include an allowance for lost profits in the damages you award if there is some reasonable basis in the evidence for finding that the plaintiff has in fact suffered a loss of profits, even though the amount of such loss is difficult to calculate.

In arriving at the amount of any lost profits the plaintiff sustained, you may consider all evidence in the case bearing upon the issue, including the plaintiff's past earnings in the business.

6.2

(SECTION 1—PER SE VIOLATION)

TYING AGREEMENT—DEFENSE OF JUSTIFICATION

[Note: Tying agreements are highly fact-specific. This suggested charge is a sample of a common tying arrangement.]

The plaintiff claims that the defendant violated the anti-trust laws of the United States.[1]

The plaintiff claims that the defendant violated antitrust laws by using a "tying" arrangement in its business with the plaintiff.

A tying arrangement is an agreement by one party to sell a product or service (known as the "tying" product) but only on the condition that the buyer also purchases a different product (known as the "tied" product) from the seller. To establish his claim, the plaintiff must prove each of the following five elements by a preponderance of the evidence:

The first element is that ___ (the "tying" product) and ___ (the "tied" product) are separate and distinct products, and not simply two components of one product.

(Sample)

The plaintiff claims that the franchise and the method of doing business that it represents, including the right to use the defendant's licensed trademark, is the "tying" product. The plaintiff also claims that the merchandise and other items manufactured or sold by the defendant constitute the second or "tied" products.

---

[1]. The judge may want to insert here the paragraph accompanying footnote 1 in Section 6.1.

6.2 PATTERN JURY INSTRUCTIONS

The defendant contends that its franchise agreement with the plaintiff was merely a system for distributing its trademarked products, that the sale of trademarked products was the primary purpose of the business to be operated under the franchise, and that the franchise or license agreement did not itself constitute a "product" that can be separated or distinguished from the distribution and sale of the trademarked goods.

A franchise or licensing agreement may be a separate product or "tying" item. You must determine whether the franchise or licensing agreement in this case was such a separate "tying" product.

The second element of the plaintiff's claim is that there was a contract or agreement in which the defendant agreed to sell ___ the "tying" product, on the condition that the plaintiff also purchase ___ the "tied" product.

The third element is that ___ had sufficient economic power or significant market leverage in the [describe relevant geographic or product market] to restrain free competition in the market for [*the tying product*].

(Sample)

The existence of a registered trademark in association with the alleged "tying" product gives rise to a presumption that the product does possess economic power or significant market leverage because, under the trademark laws, no one else may sell the goods bearing that trademark without permission of the owner of the mark.

However, the defendant contends that notwithstanding the presumption of economic

74

power, the trademark did not in fact enjoy any economic power or significant market leverage in the [*describe relevant geographic or product market*] enabling them to use the trademark as an effective means of restraining competition in the market for the "tied" products. To overcome the presumption favoring the plaintiff on this issue, the defendant must prove its contention by a preponderance of the evidence.

The fourth element of the plaintiff's claim is that the alleged tying arrangement foreclosed a "substantial volume of commerce." In deciding this question, you must look to the total dollar volume of sales in interstate commerce by the defendant to the plaintiff of the products, if any, that you find to have been tied to [*the tying product*].

The fifth element of plaintiff's claim is that it suffered injury to its business or property as a proximate result of the defendant's making an illegal "tying" agreement. The injury must have been a direct and natural consequence of the illegal "tying" arrangement.

If you find that the plaintiff has established each of these five elements of its anti-trust claim, your verdict must be for the plaintiff, unless you find that the defendant has proved a defense to the plaintiff's claim by a preponderance of the evidence. The defense the defendant claims is justification.

(Sample)

There may be a legitimate justification for an otherwise illegal "tying" arrangement. One such possible justification arises from the duties the law imposes upon a trademark owner. As the owner of the trademark [*insert name of trademark*] the defendant had a duty to the public to assure that the trademark continued to represent what it purported to represent, and that the products bearing the trademark were genuine and not of inferior quality.

On the other hand, the use of a "tying" arrangement as an alleged means of protecting a trademark and preventing its misuse is justified only in the absence of any other, less restrictive, alternative means of doing so.

Similarly, an otherwise illegal "tying" arrangement also may be justified if it is used as a necessary means for establishing a new business. A franchisor may impose restrictions on purchasing and other practices by its franchisees at the beginning of its business, and for a reasonable time thereafter, to establish good will and gain customer recognition in the market. The use of a "tying" arrangement for this purpose may be justified only if it was necessary to accomplish that purpose and there was no other, less restrictive, way of accomplishing the same objective.

If you find for the plaintiff on its anti-trust claim, and against the defendant on its affirmative defenses, you must consider the issue of damages. Proof of an antitrust violation does not necessarily mean the plaintiff was damaged. Proof of antitrust violation and antitrust injury must be shown independently.

A violation of the antitrust laws does not give rise to a right of recovery unless the plaintiff proves, by a preponderance of the evidence, that it was injured in its business or property as a proximate result of such violation. The plaintiff is not entitled to recover any losses it suffered because of poor business practices or management, unfavorable business conditions generally, or other such causes.

As to the amount of damages, the plaintiff need not prove the exact or precise amount with mathematical

ANTITRUST 6.2

certainty. But the plaintiff is not entitled to an award of damages based upon speculation or conjecture. You should award an amount shown by a preponderance of the evidence to be a sum sufficient to fairly compensate the plaintiff for the injury sustained. You may take into consideration the following elements: [*Enumerate recoverable elements of damage with explanation, as appropriate, of terms used in describing each element.*]

*

7. SECURITIES ACT

WESTLAW Electronic Research

See WESTLAW Electronic Research Guide preceding the Table of Contents.

7.1

SECURITIES ACT

(RULE 10b–5)

The plaintiff claims that the defendant violated the federal securities law.

To win, the plaintiff must establish each of the following elements by a preponderance of the evidence:

1. That the defendant used an instrumentality of interstate commerce in connection with the securities transaction involved in this case;
2. That the defendant made a misrepresentation of material fact [or failed to state a material fact] in connection with the securities transactions involved in this case;
3. That the defendant acted knowingly;
4. That the plaintiff justifiably relied upon the defendant's conduct; and
5. That the plaintiff suffered damages as a result of the defendant's wrongful conduct.

As to the first element, the use of an "instrumentality of interstate commerce" means, for example, the use of the mails or the telephone. It is not necessary that a misrepresentation or omission occur during the use of the mail or the telephone. All that is required is that the mails or the telephone be used in some phase of the transaction. In other words, it is not necessary that the misrepresentation be communicated by telephone or by mail, only that the telephone or mails be used at some stage of the events involved.

As to the second element, the alleged misrepresentations [or omissions] asserted by the plaintiff are:

[Describe the specific statements or omissions claimed to have been fraudulently made.]

To establish this second element of his claim the plaintiff must prove both

1. That the defendant made one or more misrepresentations of fact [or omitted to state facts which would be necessary to prevent the defendant's other statements from being misleading to the plaintiff] and

2. That the misrepresentation [or omission] involved "material" facts.

A "misrepresentation" is a statement that is not true.

A "material" fact [or omission] is a fact relating to a matter that would be of some importance to the reasonable investor when deciding how to invest. A minor or trivial detail is not material.

To establish the third element—that the defendant acted knowingly—the plaintiff does not satisfy the burden of proof merely by showing that the defendant acted accidentally or that the defendant made a mistake. The plaintiff must show that the defendant acted with an intent to deceive, manipulate or defraud. In other words, the plaintiff must show that the defendant stated material facts he knew to be false [or stated untrue facts with reckless disregard for their truth or falsity] [or knew of the existence of material facts that were not disclosed although he knew that knowledge of those facts would be necessary to prevent his other statements from being misleading].

To satisfy the fourth element of the plaintiff's claim—justifiable reliance—the plaintiff must prove that he in fact relied upon the false statements. If you find that the plaintiff would have engaged in the transaction anyway, and that the misrepresentation had no effect upon his decision, then there was no reliance and plaintiff loses. Also, the plaintiff must prove that his reliance was justified. The plaintiff cannot have intentionally closed his eyes and refused to investigate the circumstances in disregard of a risk known to him, or a risk that was so obvious that he should have been aware of it, and so great as to make it highly probable that harm would follow.

[If you find that the defendant made an omission or failed to disclose a material fact, you must presume that the plaintiff relied upon the omission or failure to disclose. The defendant may rebut this presumption if he proves, by a preponderance of the evidence, that even if the material fact had been disclosed, the plaintiff's decision as to the transaction would not have been different.]

As to the fifth element—damages—the plaintiff must show that his damages were a proximate result of the misrepresentation [or omission]. He must show that, except for the misrepresentation [or omission] such damage would not have occurred.

If you find for the plaintiff on his claim, you must then consider the issue of the amount of money damages to award to the plaintiff. You should award the plaintiff an amount of money shown by a preponderance of the evidence to be fair and adequate compensation for the loss that proximately resulted from the defendant's wrongful conduct.

[*Enumerate recoverable elements of damage with explanation, as appropriate, of the terms used in describing each element.*]

*

8. RICO

WESTLAW Electronic Research
See WESTLAW Electronic Research Guide preceding the Table of Contents.

8.1

RICO CLAIMS

The plaintiff has brought claims against each defendant for alleged violations of the Racketeer Influenced and Corrupt Organizations Act, commonly referred to as RICO. Specifically, the plaintiff claims that each defendant violated Section 1962 [(a) (b) (c) or (d)] of RICO.

The plaintiff must establish by a preponderance of the evidence every element of a RICO claim. You should consider each and every element of a RICO cause of action only in the precise way that I will define them in these instructions. You must avoid confusing any of the elements of a RICO claim with your prior conceptions of the meaning of the terms that are used to describe the elements of a RICO claim.

SECTION 1962(a)

I. The plaintiff has alleged that each defendant violated Section 1962(a) of the RICO Act. To establish that a defendant violated Section 1962(a), the plaintiff must prove by a preponderance of the evidence each of the following four elements:

1. That there was an "enterprise";
2. That the enterprise engaged in or had some effect "on interstate commerce";
3. That the defendant derived income, directly or indirectly, from a "pattern of racketeering activity"; and

8.1 PATTERN JURY INSTRUCTIONS

4. That some part of that income was used in acquiring an interest in or operating the enterprise.

A "person" under the law includes but is not limited to any person or entity that is capable of holding a legal or beneficial interest in property. A corporation is a legal entity that, like a person, is capable of holding a legal or beneficial interest in property.

The term "enterprise" includes any individual, partnership, corporation, association, or other legal entity. An enterprise "affects interstate or foreign commerce" if the enterprise either engages in, or has an effect on commerce between the states or between the states and foreign countries.

A "racketeering activity" means an act in violation of [(the federal mail fraud statute) (the federal wire fraud statute) (securities fraud statutes).] You will be instructed on the law pertaining to this (these) statute(s) to guide you in determining whether the plaintiff proved by a preponderance of the evidence that a defendant committed one or more violations of these statutes. A "racketeering activity" may also be referred to as a "predicate offense".

A "pattern of racketeering activity" requires that the plaintiff prove that a defendant committed at least two acts of "racketeering activity" within ten years of each other [and that both of the acts occurred after October 15, 1970.] The proof of two or more predicate acts does not in and of itself establish a "pattern" under RICO. The two acts need not be of the same kind. For example, the acts may be one act of mail fraud and one act of wire fraud. However, you must find by a preponderance of the evidence that the two acts occurred within the time specified and that each was connected with the other by some common scheme, plan or motive so as to constitute a "pattern". A series of wholly separate, isolated or disconnected acts of racketeering activity does not constitute a pattern.

In other words, two or more otherwise unrelated acts of "racketeering activity" do not constitute a "pattern" of racketeering activity under RICO unless the acts all relate to a common scheme by the defendant to continually conduct the affairs of the alleged enterprise for illicit personal benefit, whether monetary or otherwise, for himself or for another, by committing the predicate offenses.

As I instructed you, "racketeering activity" means an act in violation of [the mail fraud and/or wire fraud and/or securities fraud statutes.] However you may not consider just any racketeering act allegedly committed by a defendant in violation of one of these statutes as bearing on the question of whether a defendant has committed two or more predicate offenses as a pattern of racketeering activity. In making this determination, you are to consider only those specific racketeering acts alleged by the plaintiff against a particular defendant. Furthermore, you cannot find that the defendant has engaged in a "pattern of racketeering activity" unless you unanimously agree to which of the alleged predicate offenses, if any, make up the pattern. Thus, it would not be sufficient if some of you should find that a defendant committed a violation of two or more predicate offenses under one particular statute as a pattern and the rest of you should find that a defendant committed a violation of two or more predicate acts under another statute as a pattern. In other words, you may not find that the defendant has engaged in a pattern of racketeering activity unless you [1] find a "pattern" of predicate offenses and [2] find that the plaintiff has proved by a preponderance of the evidence that a defendant committed each of the two or more predicate offenses that you find are necessary to make up the pattern.

8.1 PATTERN JURY INSTRUCTIONS

You should note that the pattern must be one in which the defendant has participated as a "principal." Thus in order to satisfy the second element, the plaintiff must prove the defendant was a "principal" by showing by a preponderance of the evidence:

1. That the defendant knowingly and willfully committed, or knowingly and willfully aided and abetted in the commission of two or more alleged predicate offenses that constitute the alleged pattern of racketeering activity, and

2. That the defendant knowingly and willfully received income derived, directly or indirectly, from that alleged pattern of racketeering activity.

The word "knowingly," as that term has been used in these instructions, means that the action was done voluntarily and intentionally and not because of mistake or accident.

The word "willfully," as that term has been used in these instructions, means that the action was committed voluntarily and purposely, with the specific intent to do something the law forbids. The action must be done with a bad purpose: either to disobey or disregard the law.

The plaintiff has alleged that each of the defendants has committed two or more predicate acts including violations of the mail fraud and wire fraud statutes. It is your function to decide whether the plaintiff has proved by a preponderance of the evidence as to each defendant whether that defendant violated either or both of those statutes on one or more occasions, if at all. To establish that mail fraud has been committed, the plaintiff must prove each of the following by a preponderance of the evidence as to each defendant so charged:

1. Some person or persons willfully and knowingly devised a scheme or artifice to defraud, or a

scheme for obtaining money or property by means of false pretenses, representations or promises, and

2. Some person or persons used the United States Postal Service by mailing, or by causing to be mailed, some matter or thing for the purpose of executing the scheme to defraud.

To act with "intent to defraud" means to act knowingly and with the specific intent to deceive. The words "scheme" and "artifice" in the mail fraud statute include any plan or course of action intended to deceive others, and to obtain property by false or fraudulent pretenses, representations, or promises, from the persons so deceived.

A statement or representation is "false" or "fraudulent" within the meaning of the mail fraud statute if it relates to a material fact and is known to be untrue or is made with reckless indifference as to its truth or falsity, and is made or caused to be made with intent to defraud. A statement or representation may also be "false" or "fraudulent" if it constitutes a half truth, or effectively conceals a material fact, with intent to defraud. A material fact is a fact that would be important to a reasonable person in deciding whether to engage in a particular transaction.

Good faith constitutes a complete defense to mail fraud. Good faith means the actor had a genuine belief that the information which was sent or given was true.

The plaintiff must prove by a preponderance of the evidence that one or more of the defendants knowingly and willfully devised or intended to devise a scheme to defraud which was substantially the same as the one alleged by the plaintiff and that the use of the United States Mail was closely related to the scheme in that one or more of the defendants either mailed something or caused it to be mailed in an attempt to execute or carry out the scheme. One causes the mails to be used if he does an act with knowledge that the use of the mails will follow in the ordinary course of business, or if he can reasonably foresee such use.

To establish that wire fraud has been committed, the plaintiff must prove by a preponderance of the evidence that the defendant used the telephone (telegraph) for the purpose of executing the scheme to defraud.

To establish wire fraud, it must be found that when the defendant performed an act, he knew, or reasonably could foresee, that the telephone or telegraph would be used to further a scheme or artifice to defraud.

With respect to the fourth element of Section 1962(a) of the RICO Act—use of income to acquire an interest in, establish or operate an enterprise—you must decide whether a defendant, directly or indirectly, used any part of the income derived from a pattern of racketeering activity to acquire an interest in, to establish, or to operate the alleged enterprise. The plaintiff must prove by a preponderance of the evidence that a defendant, or any of them, invested income in a specific enterprise and that income was acquired through the scheme in which they illegally used the mails (telephone) with respect to that particular alleged enterprise.

The plaintiff claims that each of the following is an enterprise which affects interstate or foreign commerce, and that each defendant participated in each alleged enterprise through a separate and distinct pattern of racketeering activity:

[*Describe enterprise allegations here*]

SECTION 1962(b)

II. The plaintiff also claims that the defendants have violated Section 1962(b) of RICO. To establish a violation of Section 1962(b), the plaintiff must prove by a preponderance of the evidence each one of the following four elements:

1. That an enterprise existed;
2. That the enterprise engaged in or had some effect upon interstate or foreign commerce;
3. That the defendant engaged in a pattern of racketeering activity; and
4. That through the pattern of racketeering activity the defendant acquired or maintained an interest in, or controlled the alleged enterprise.

[I have already instructed you about the first three elements of Section (b) in the previous discussion of Section (a). If you find that the alleged enterprise existed and engaged in or had some effect upon interstate or foreign commerce, and that the defendant engaged in a pattern of racketeering activity, then you must consider the fourth element.]

This fourth element that plaintiff must prove by a preponderance of the evidence is that the defendants, or any of them, through the pattern of racketeering activity, acquired or maintained an interest in, or control of one or more of the alleged enterprises. To find that the plaintiff established this fourth element, you must find by a preponderance of the evidence not only that the defendants, or any of them, had some interest in or control over one or more of the alleged enterprises, but also that this interest or control was associated with or connected to the pattern of racketeering activity.

SECTION 1962(c)

III. The plaintiff also has alleged that defendants have violated Section 1962(c) of RICO. To establish that the defendant has violated Section 1962(c), the plaintiff must prove each of the following five elements by a preponderance of the evidence:

1. That an "enterprise" existed [1];

---

1. Under Section 1962(c), the RICO "person" and the RICO "enterprise" cannot be one and the same. However, under Sections 1962(a) and

8.1 **PATTERN JURY INSTRUCTIONS**

2. That the enterprise engaged in, or had some effect upon, interstate or foreign commerce;
3. That the defendant was employed by or associated with the alleged enterprise;
4. That the defendant knowingly and willfully conducted or participated, directly or indirectly, in the conduct of the affairs of the alleged enterprise; and
5. That the defendant did so knowingly and willfully through a pattern of racketeering activity.

"Employed by or associated with" means some minimal association with the alleged enterprise. The defendant must know something about the alleged enterprise's activities as they relate to the racketeering activity.

The fourth and fifth elements require that the plaintiff prove by a preponderance of the evidence that the defendant knowingly and willfully conducted or participated in the conducting of the affairs of the alleged enterprise through a pattern of racketeering activity. The plaintiff must prove by a preponderance of the evidence a sufficient connection between the enterprise, the defendant, and the alleged pattern of racketeering activity. In order to establish a sufficient connection between the enterprise, the defendant and the alleged pattern of racketeering activity, the plaintiff must prove by a preponderance of the evidence:

1. That the defendant participated in the operation or management of the enterprise itself in

---

(b), "enterprise" and "person" may be the same and need not be separate and distinct. In re Burzynski, 989 F.2d 733 (5th Cir.1993); Landry v. Air Line Pilots Association, et al., 901 F.2d 404 (5th Cir.1990). *See also,* Liquid Air Corporation v. Rogers, et al., 834 F.2d 1297 (7th Cir.1987); Petro-Tech, Inc. v. The Western Company of North America, 824 F.2d 1349 (3d Cir.1987); Haroco v. American National Bank and Trust Company of Chicago, et al., 747 F.2d 384 (7th Cir.1984); Bowman v. Western Auto Supply Company, et al., 773 F.Supp. 174 (W.D.Mo.1991); Harrison v. Dean Witter Reynolds, Inc., et al., 695 F.Supp. 959 (N.D.Ill.1988).

such a way, directly or indirectly, as to have played some part in directing the affairs of the enterprise.[2]

2. That the defendant in fact engaged in the pattern of racketeering activity as the plaintiff claims;

3. That the defendant's association with or employment by the enterprise facilitated his commission of the racketeering acts; and

4. That the commission of these predicate acts had some direct or indirect effect on the alleged enterprise.

A person does not violate the law by merely associating with or being employed by an otherwise lawful enterprise the affairs of which are being conducted by others through a pattern of racketeering activity in which he is not personally engaged.

SECTION 1962(d)

IV. Plaintiff also claims that the defendants violated Section 1962(d) of RICO because the defendants agreed or conspired to violate the RICO law.

A "conspiracy" in this sense is a combination or agreement of two or more persons to join together to accomplish an offense which would be in violation of Section 1962(a), (b), and/or (c) under the law that I have given you with respect to those sections.

To establish a violation of Section 1962(d), the plaintiff must prove by a preponderance of the evidence:

1. That two or more persons in some way or manner came to a mutual understanding to

---

2. The United States Supreme Court adopted the "operation and management" test of the Eighth Circuit in defining the scope of the meaning of "to conduct or participate . . . in the conduct of such enterprise's affairs through a pattern of racketeering activity." Reves v. Ernst & Young, 507 U.S. 170, 113 S.Ct. 1163, 122 L.Ed.2d 525 (1993).

attempt to accomplish a common and unlawful plan, that is that while being employed by or associated with an enterprise, they engaged in activities which affected interstate or foreign commerce, or conducted the affairs of the alleged enterprise through a pattern of racketeering activity, in the manner charged; and

2. That the defendant knowingly and willfully became a member of a conspiracy by objectively indicating, through his words or actions, his agreement to conduct or participate, directly or indirectly, in the conduct of the affairs of an enterprise through a pattern of racketeering activity; and

3. That at least one of the conspirators committed at least one overt act during the existence of a conspiracy in an effort to accomplish some object or purpose of the conspiracy.

The definitions and instructions that I gave to you earlier as to "enterprise," "racketeering activity," "pattern of racketeering activity," "conduct through a pattern of racketeering activity" and "engaged in, or the activities of which affect, interstate or foreign commerce" apply here.

In regard to the first element of the claim of conspiracy, the evidence in the case need not show that the alleged members of the conspiracy entered into any express or formal agreement, or that they directly stated between themselves the details of the scheme and its object or purpose or the precise means by which the object or purpose was to be accomplished. Similarly, the evidence in the case need not establish that all of the means or methods alleged were in fact set forth in the indictment were in fact agreed upon to carry out the alleged conspiracy, or that all of the means or methods which were agreed upon were actually used or put into operation. The plaintiff is not required to prove that all

RICO 8.1

of the persons charged with being members of the conspiracy were such or that the alleged conspirators actually succeeded in accomplishing their unlawful objectives.

On the other hand, it is not enough if the evidence shows only that the alleged conspirators agreed to commit the acts of racketeering alleged by the plaintiff, without more, or that they agreed merely to participate in the affairs of the same alleged enterprise. Instead, the plaintiff must prove by a preponderance of the evidence that the alleged conspirators agreed to conduct or participate in the conduct of the affairs of the alleged enterprise and that they further agreed that their individual participations would be through two or more racketeering acts in furtherance of the affairs of the alleged enterprise. It does not matter that the alleged conspirators participated in the conduct of the affairs of the alleged enterprise through different, dissimilar or otherwise unrelated acts of racketeering activity, so long as the alleged racketeering acts would, if they were actually committed, create a "pattern of racketeering activity" as I defined that phrase to you.

As to the second element of the alleged conspiracy violation—knowing and willful membership in the conspiracy—the plaintiff must prove by a preponderance of the evidence:

1. That the defendant knew that the basic object of the alleged conspiracy was conducting the alleged enterprise through a pattern of racketeering activity;
2. That the defendant knowingly and willfully agreed to personally commit, or aid and abet the commission of at least two acts of racketeering as a "pattern of racketeering activity" as I have defined it; and
3. That the defendant knowingly and willfully agreed to conduct or participate in the conduct

8.1 PATTERN JURY INSTRUCTIONS

of the affairs of the alleged enterprise through this pattern of racketeering activity.

One may become a member of a conspiracy without full knowledge of all of the details of the unlawful scheme or without knowledge of the names and identities of all of the other alleged conspirators. If the plaintiff proves by a preponderance of the evidence that the particular defendant has knowingly and willfully joined the alleged conspiracy under the three standards I have just set forth, it does not matter that the defendant may not have participated in the earlier stages of the alleged conspiracy or scheme.

However, mere presence at the scene of some transaction or event, or mere similarity of conduct among various persons and the fact that they may have associated with each other, and may have assembled together and discussed common aims and interests, does not necessarily prove the existence of a conspiracy. Also, a person who has no knowledge of a conspiracy, but who happens to act in a way which advances some object or purpose of a conspiracy, does not thereby become a conspirator.

The plaintiff need not prove that the defendant actually committed any of the acts that he may have agreed to commit in order to establish his membership in the conspiracy. You may consider only those racketeering acts alleged against the particular defendant by the plaintiff in determining whether that defendant has agreed to commit two acts of racketeering activity as a "pattern of racketeering activity." [These alleged racketeering acts are outlined as to each defendant on pages ___ of these instructions.]

To establish the third element, the plaintiff must prove by a preponderance of the evidence that at least one of the alleged conspirators committed at least one "overt act" during the existence of the alleged conspiracy. An "overt act" is a transaction or event, even one which may be entirely legal and innocent when considered alone, but which is knowingly committed by a conspirator in an effort to accomplish some object of the conspiracy. However, in accordance with my instructions during the trial, you may not consider any evidence of any alleged wrongful act, other than the alleged wrongful act which the plaintiff contends is a specific violation, as in any way bearing on the character of any defendant or as an indication that any defendant may have a propensity to commit any of the offenses charged.

In your consideration of this conspiracy claim, you should first determine whether the alleged conspiracy existed. If you conclude that a conspiracy did exist as alleged, you should next determine whether or not the defendant under consideration willfully became a member of that conspiracy.

In determining whether there was a conspiracy you may consider all the evidence in the case. If you find that there was a conspiracy then you may attribute the statements or acts of the _____, [insert names of co-conspirators] to the defendant. If you find that there was no conspiracy then you may not attribute the statements or acts of _____, [insert names of alleged co-conspirators] to the defendant.[1]

If you find that no such conspiracy existed, then you must find for the defendants. However, if you are satisfied that such a conspiracy existed, you must determine who were the members of that conspiracy.

If you find that a particular defendant is a member of another conspiracy, but not the one charged by the

1. Bourjaily v. United States, 483 U.S. 171, 107 S.Ct. 2775, 97 L.Ed.2d 144 (1987). Under Bourjaily in a criminal case the court must consider as a preliminary matter under Federal Rule of Evidence 104 whether or not a conspiracy existed based on a preponderance of the evidence before it decides whether or not to admit co-conspirators' statements as substantive evidence under 801. Once the evidence comes in it seems that the jury may consider it for whatever purpose it desires.

8.1 PATTERN JURY INSTRUCTIONS

plaintiff, then you must find for that defendant. In other words, you cannot find that a defendant violated Section 1962(d) unless you find that he was a member of the conspiracy charged, and not some other separate conspiracy.

CAUSATION

Finally, for the plaintiff to prevail under RICO, he must prove by a preponderance of the evidence that the defendant's RICO violations were the "proximate cause" of injury to the plaintiff's business or property. Therefore you must find that the plaintiff suffered an injury to his business or property and that the injury was caused by reason of the defendants' violation of RICO.

An injury or damage is proximately caused when the act played a substantial part in bringing about or actually causing injury or damage, and that the injury or damage was either a direct result or a reasonably probable consequence of the act.

A person is injured in his business when he suffers loss of money or profits or a reduction in the value or worth of his business.

A finding that the plaintiff was injured in his business or property because of the defendant's violation of RICO requires only that you find the plaintiff was harmed by the predicate acts.

However, to find that injury to the plaintiff's business or property was caused by reason of the defendants' violation of RICO, you must find that the injury to the plaintiff was caused by, and was a direct result of the defendants' violation of either Section 1962(a) or (b) or (c).

Therefore, you must find that the commission of the acts of racketeering, or the pattern of racketeering activity, or the conduct of the affairs of the enterprise through the pattern of racketeering activity directly resulted in the injury or played a substantial role in producing the injury.

In considering the issue of damages, if any, with respect to the RICO claims, you must assess the amount you find justified by a preponderance of the evidence as full, just and reasonable compensation for all of the damages to the plaintiff in his business or property. Damages may not be based on speculation because it is only actual damages (what the law calls compensatory damages) that you are to determine.

You should consider the amount of damages, if any, as to each defendant with respect to each RICO claim separately and independently from the amount of damages, if any, with respect to the other, non-RICO claims. For example, and by way of example only, if you determine that damages should be awarded to the plaintiff under his RICO claim, you should award full, just and reasonable compensation for damages under the RICO claim, without regard to the damages, if any, you might award under any other claim brought by the plaintiff.

The fact that I have given you instructions concerning the issue of the plaintiff's damages should not be interpreted in any way as an indication that I believe that the plaintiff should or should not prevail in this case. The interrogatories which you will answer contain several questions about damages under different laws and different theories of recovery. You should not draw any inference from the fact that a damage question has been asked. You must answer each Interrogatory separately and award damages, if appropriate, independently of damages which you may award under any other interrogatory.

SUGGESTED RICO JURY INTERROGATORIES

NOTE: These special interrogatories for RICO claims are provided as illustrations and guide-

8.1 PATTERN JURY INSTRUCTIONS

lines to assist in preparation of special interrogatories for other claims.

SPECIAL ISSUE NO. 1

Do you find from a preponderance of the evidence that any defendant received any income derived, directly or indirectly, from a pattern of racketeering activity in which that defendant participated as a principal, and that the defendant used or invested, directly or indirectly, any part of that income, to acquire an interest in, establish, or operate an enterprise which is engaged in, or the activities of which affect, interstate commerce?

Answer as to each defendant and each enterprise.

SPECIAL ISSUE NO. 2

What sum of money, if any, do you find from a preponderance of the evidence would reasonably compensate the plaintiff for actual damages, if any, to his business or property proximately caused by the operation of an enterprise, if any you have so found, through a pattern of racketeering activity, if any you have so found?

Answer separately as to each defendant and enterprise.

SPECIAL ISSUE NO. 3

Do you find from a preponderance of the evidence that any defendant listed below, through a pattern of racketeering activity, acquired or maintained, directly or indirectly, any interest in or control of any enterprise which is engaged in, or the activities of which affect, interstate or foreign commerce?

Answer yes or no as to each defendant.

SPECIAL ISSUE NO. 4

What sum of money, if any, do you find from a preponderance of the evidence would reasonably compensate the plaintiff for actual damages, if any, to his business or property arising from any of the defendants' acquisition or maintenance of each enterprise?

Answer separately as to each defendant and enterprise.

SPECIAL ISSUE NO. 5

Do you find from a preponderance of the evidence that any defendant listed below was employed by or associated with an enterprise engaged in, or the activities of which affected, interstate or foreign commerce?

Answer as to each defendant and each enterprise.

SPECIAL ISSUE NO. 6

What sum of money, if any, do you find from a preponderance of the evidence would reasonably compensate the plaintiff for actual damages to his business or property arising from any defendant's employment by or association with each enterprise, if any you have so found?

Answer separately as to each defendant and each enterprise.

SPECIAL ISSUE NO. 7

Do you find from a preponderance of the evidence that any defendant entered into a conspiracy with any other person to accomplish any of the purposes described below?

Answer yes or no separately as to each category and defendant.

> 1. To receive income derived, directly or indirectly, from a pattern of racketeering activity in which at least one of the defendants participated as a principal, to use or invest, directly or indirectly any part of such income, or the proceeds of such income, in an acquisition of any interest in, or the establishment or operation of, any enterprise which is en-

gaged in or the activities of which affects interstate or foreign commerce.

2. To acquire or maintain through a pattern of racketeering activity any interest in or control, directly or indirectly, of any enterprise which is engaged in, or the activities of which affects interstate or foreign commerce.

3. To conduct or participate, directly or indirectly, in the conduct of the affairs of an enterprise which is engaged in, or the activities of which affect, interstate commerce or foreign commerce through a pattern of racketeering activity, while employed by or associated with such enterprise.

9. PATENT INFRINGEMENT

WESTLAW Electronic Research

See WESTLAW Electronic Research Guide preceding the Table of Contents.

9.1

PATENT INFRINGEMENT

This is a patent infringement suit. The plaintiff claims that the defendant infringed a patent that the plaintiff owned. The plaintiff also claims that the defendant has caused others to infringe the plaintiff's patent. The plaintiff seeks damages for patent infringement from the time the patent was issued to the present time.

Once a patent is issued, the owner of the patent has the right to exclude others from making, using or selling the patented invention throughout the United States for a term of seventeen years. Thus, infringement of a patent occurs whenever any person, without the owner's permission, makes, uses or sells the patented invention anywhere in the United States, while the patent is in force.

The application for a patent must be in writing, under oath or written declaration, and often must contain a drawing, and a specification containing a written description of the invention and of the manner and process of making and using it. This is called the claims of the patent. These claims define the exact limits or nature of the invention, and it is only the claims of the patent that can be infringed.[1] In this case,

---

1. In prior editions, the model jury charge for patent infringement instructed jurors that specifications and drawings could be used to explain

9.1 PATTERN JURY INSTRUCTIONS

the plaintiff contends that the defendant infringed upon claim nos. [*list claim numbers*] of patent no. [*insert patent number*]:

[insert patent claims]

Plaintiff may prove its claim of infringement by demonstrating either that the defendant's [product/process] literally infringes a claim contained in patent or that the accused [product/process] infringes one of the patent claims under the doctrine of equivalents.[2]

A [product/process] literally infringes a claim of a patent when it contains each and every element of the invention as defined by the particular patent claim. In other words, a [product/process] literally infringes a patent claim when the same combination of [steps/elements] found in the claim can also be found in the [process/product]. In making your determination, you must therefore consider each claim separately. If you find that it has been proven by a preponderance of the evidence that the accused [product/process] contains every element of a particular claim in the plaintiff's patent, the defendant has literally infringed that claim. On the other hand, if you find that plaintiff has not proven by a preponderance of the evidence that the accused [product/process] contains every element of a particular claim, the patent claim has not been literally infringed.

the meaning of words used in claims. This language has been deleted because the meaning and scope of claims are questions of law for the court. See Markman v. Westview Instruments, Inc., 52 F.3d 967 (Fed.Cir.1995) (en banc). The Supreme Court granted writs in this case. See ___ U.S. ___, 116 S.Ct. 40, 132 L.Ed.2d 921 (1995).

2. A party asserting infringement under the doctrine of equivalents must present evidence establishing what the function, way, and result of both the claimed device and the accused device are, and why those functions, ways, and results are substantially the same, to be entitled to have the issue presented to the jury. See Lear Siegler, Inc. v. Sealy Mattress Co., 873 F.2d 1422, 1426–27 (Fed.Cir.1989).

PATENT INFRINGEMENT 9.1

Even though each and every [step/element] of a particular claim does not appear in the defendant's [product/process], the patent claim may still have been infringed, if you determine that the defendant's [product/process] is substantially equivalent to the patent claim. This is called infringement under the doctrine of equivalents. Under the doctrine, the defendant's [product/process] infringes a patent claim if it performs substantially the same function in substantially the same way to produce substantially the same result as the [steps/elements] recited in the claim. On the other hand, defendant's [product/process] does not infringe a patent claim under the doctrine of equivalents if it is so far changed in principle that it performs the same function in a substantially different way as the [steps/elements] recited in the claim. In other words, for there to be an infringement under the doctrine of equivalents, you must determine that plaintiff has proven by a preponderance of the evidence not only that the defendant's [product/process] performs substantially the same function to achieve substantially the same result as the plaintiff's invention, but also the presence, in the accused device, of every claim element or its substantial equivalent. You should view the evidence from the perspective of a person of ordinary skill in the art. The test is objective, that is, whether a person of ordinary skill in the art would have considered the differences insubstantial.

A factor to consider is whether there is evidence of known interchangeability of the accused and claimed elements. If a person with ordinary skill in the art would have known about the interchangeability of the accused and claimed elements, you may infer that such a person would have considered the change insubstantial.

You may also consider evidence of copying. If you find that the defendant has attempted to copy the patented invention, you may infer that the defendant has made a fair copy with only insubstantial changes. On the other hand, if you find that the defendant was attempting to "design around" the patent, that is, that the defendant used the patent to design a new [product/process] that does not infringe, you may infer that the defendant has designed substantial changes into the new [product/process] to avoid infringement. However, an inference is just that, an inference. An inference is not conclusive, and it is for you to decide the strength of the inference based on the strength of the evidence supporting it. Moreover, in reaching a conclusion on the issue of infringement under the doctrine of equivalents, you must weigh any inference together with the other evidence of the substantiality of the differences.

I instruct you that a person who has developed his product or process through independent research has not "designed around" the patent because an independent developer without knowledge could not have set out to make his [product/process] different from the claimed device. By the same token, if the accused [product/process] was developed through independent research or the inventor had no knowledge of the patent, you should find that the defendant did not copy the patent since he could not have set out to make his [product/process] similar to the claimed device. However, independent development or the absence of bad faith on the part of the defendant is not excuse for infringement. Those who make only insubstantial changes to a patented product or process are liable for infringement regardless of their awareness of the patent and its disclosure.[3]

---

3. In Hilton-Davis Chemical Co. v. Warner–Jenkinson Co., 62 F.3d 1512 (Fed.Cir.1995), the Federal Circuit recognized that the traditional function-way-result test is often adequate for resolving "equivalency" issues. However, the court also recognized that as "technology becomes more sophisticated and the innovative process more complex, the functional-way-result test may not invariably suffice to show the substantiality of differences." Accordingly, when the record presents other evidence of substantiality, the court should instruct the fact-finder to consider it. If there is no evidence

PATENT INFRINGEMENT 9.1

In your deliberations on the issue of infringement, you are instructed not to interpret or construe the meaning or the scope of the claims. Your decision should be based solely on a comparison of the defendant's [product/process] with the plaintiff's patent claims as they are hereinafter defined. Claim [*insert patent claim number*] of plaintiff's patent is composed of the following elements[4]:

[Define Plaintiff's Patent Claims.]

In your deliberations, you should consider the issue of literal infringement first. If you find that the defendant's [product/process] does not literally infringe a particular claim, you should then consider whether the accused [product/process] infringes that claim under the doctrine of equivalents. On the other hand, if you determine that defendant's [product/process] literally infringes a particular claim, you should then move on to the next claim allegedly infringed by the accused [product/process] without considering the issue of infringement under the doctrine of equivalents. If you find that the plaintiff has failed to prove by a preponderance of the evidence that the defendant infringed any of the claims listed above, either literally or under the doctrine of equivalents, you must find for the defendant. However, if you find that the plaintiff has established by a preponderance of the evidence that the defendant infringed one or more claims, you must then determine whether the patent is a valid patent.

---

of substantiality apart from function-way-result evidence, instructions on "known interchangeability," copying, and the development process are unnecessary. The precise wording of this instruction should therefore be revised by the court to reflect the evidence admitted at trial. The Supreme Court granted writs in this case. See __ U.S. __, 116 S.Ct. 1014, 134 L.Ed.2d 95 (1996).

4. The meaning and scope of the claims are questions of law for the court, and the elements of each claim and any term definitions should be provided by the court. See Markman v. Westview Instruments, Inc., 52 F.3d 967 (Fed.Cir.1995) (en banc) cert. granted, __ U.S. __, 116 S.Ct. 40, 132 L.Ed.2d 921 (1995).

9.1 PATTERN JURY INSTRUCTIONS

A patent that the United States Patent Office issues is presumed to be valid. Each claim of a patent is presumed valid independently of the validity of the other claims. The defendant must establish with clear and convincing evidence that the plaintiff's patent or any claim in the patent is not valid. Because the law presumes that the patent is valid, the defendant must come forward with something more than a preponderance of the evidence in order to overcome that presumption. However, this presumption of validity extends only to the record before the examiners in the Patent and Trademark Office in Washington. That record is called the file wrapper. Where the file wrapper discloses that the examiner considered certain information or documents during the prosecution of the application for the patent, there is a presumption that the examiner found patentable differences between the information or the documents he considered and the invention claimed in the plaintiff's patent application. However, there is no presumption of patentable differences from information or documents in the file wrapper that you find the examiner did not consider. But as to any information or documents which you find in the file wrapper that the examiner did not consider, and which you find discloses an invention more like the one claimed in the plaintiff's patent than the inventions disclosed in the information which the examiner did consider, no such presumption exists, and you may take such failure into account in deciding whether there is clear and convincing evidence which overcome or outweighs the presumption concerning the validity of the plaintiff's patent.

[When the affirmative defense asserted is a failure to disclose the prior art by the patentee, the burden is only by a preponderance of the evidence; therefore, the pattern instruction must be modified to reflect the correct burden of proof.]

A person is not entitled to a patent if:

1. The claimed invention was publicly known or used by others in the United States, or patented or described in a printed publication in the United States or in a foreign country, before the applicant allegedly invented it; or

2. The claimed invention was patented or described in a printed publication in the United States or a foreign country or was in public use or on sale in the United States, more than one year prior to the date of the application for patent in the United States; or

3. The applicant has abandoned the claimed invention; or

4. The applicant or a representative of the applicant filed a foreign patent application on the claimed invention twelve months before the United States application was filed and the foreign patent was issued before the United States application was filed; or

5. The claimed invention was described in a United States patent granted to someone else before the applicant invented it; or

6. The applicant did not personally invent the subject matter sought to be patented; or

7. Before the applicant's invention, the claimed invention was made in the United States by another who had not abandoned, suppressed or concealed it; or

8. The differences between the subject matter sought to be patented and the prior art are such that the subject matter as a whole would have been obvious, at the time the claimed invention was made, to a person having ordinary skill in the art to which said subject matter pertains.

Prior art includes all of the knowledge, acts, descriptions and patents which I have just described to

9.1 PATTERN JURY INSTRUCTIONS

you, such as public knowledge and use by others in this country, patents, and descriptions in printed publications in the United States or in a foreign country. However, the patentability of an invention does not depend on how the invention was made.

If one prior art reference completely embodies the same [process/product] as any claim of the plaintiff's patent, the [process/product] recited by that claim is said to be anticipated by the prior art and that the claim of the patent is therefore invalid for want of novelty. Similarly, if you find that the differences between the [process/product] recited in any claim in the plaintiff's patent and what is taught by the prior art would have been such that the whole idea would have been obvious to a person skilled in the field at the time the claimed invention was made, then the [process/product] is said to be "obvious" from the prior art and the claim of the patent is invalid.

The plaintiff has introduced evidence that the claimed invention filled a long felt need, that others failed in their attempts to develop it, that it has enjoyed commercial success, and that others have entered into consent decrees and have obtained licenses to manufacture the patented device. You may consider that evidence in determining whether or not the claimed invention would have been obvious if such evidence is related to features of the [process/product] claimed in the patent and not to other considerations such as advertising, promotion, salesmanship or, in the case of the prior licenses, the cost of litigation and the like.

If you find that the defendant has infringed any of the claims of the plaintiff's patent and that those claims are valid, you must then consider the issue of damages to be awarded to the plaintiff.

If you find there has been an infringement, the owner of the patent is entitled to an award of damages adequate to compensate for the infringement, but in no

PATENT INFRINGEMENT 9.1

event less than a reasonable royalty for the use made of the invention by the infringer.

This means that the minimum damages to which the plaintiff is entitled is what you determine, from a preponderance of the evidence, would have been a reasonable royalty for a license to the defendant to use the claimed invention during the period of the infringement. A reasonable royalty is the amount which the owner of a patent would accept, assuming a willingness on the owner's part to license its use, from a person who wants to obtain a license to use the claimed invention, neither of whom is acting under financial distress or other compulsion to enter into the agreement.

You must calculate damages from the moment of infringement, if all of the products manufactured and sold by the plaintiff or by persons acting under the plaintiff were properly marked, that is, the products contained the number of the patent from the time when the plaintiff obtained the patent. If not, you should calculate the damages from the time the defendant was first notified of the infringement. Filing of an action for infringement is such notice. If the products were not marked, with their patent number, then you should not award any damages for the period of time before the defendant had notice of the infringement.

However, if the defendant had actual knowledge of the plaintiff's patent and, in spite of such knowledge, willfully and wantonly made, used or sold the patented [process/product] without the permission of the plaintiff and with a disregard for the rights of the plaintiff, then you may find that the defendant is guilty of willful infringement. If you find that there was a willful infringement by the defendant then you may treble—that is, multiply by three—the amount of the damages you award.

*

10. CIVIL RIGHTS

WESTLAW Electronic Research

See WESTLAW Electronic Research Guide preceding the Table of Contents.

10.1

42 USC SECTION 1983 (UNLAWFUL ARREST—UNLAWFUL SEARCH—EXCESSIVE FORCE) QUALIFIED IMMUNITY—GOOD FAITH DEFENSE

[The plaintiff claims that the defendant(s), while acting "under color of state law," intentionally deprived the plaintiff of rights under the Constitution of the United States.]

The plaintiff claims that the defendant(s), while acting under color of authority of the State of _____ [as members of the Police Department of the City of _____] intentionally violated the plaintiff's constitutional rights. The constitutional rights that the plaintiff claims the Defendant(s) violated are these:

1. The right not to be deprived of liberty without due process of law;
2. The right not to be subjected to an unreasonable search of one's home or dwelling; and
3. The constitutional right to be free from the use of excessive force during an arrest.

Under the Constitution of the United States, a citizen has both the right to his liberty and the right not to be arrested without due process of law. He also has the right under the Constitution not to be subjected to an unreasonable search of his home; and, finally, he has the constitutional right not to be subjected to unreason-

10.1   PATTERN JURY INSTRUCTIONS

able force while being arrested by a law enforcement officer, even though the arrest is otherwise proper.

A person may sue for an award of money damages against anyone who, "under color" of any State law or custom, intentionally violates his rights under the Constitution of the United States.

The plaintiff must prove each of the following by a preponderance of the evidence:

1. That the defendant(s) intentionally committed acts that violated one or more of the plaintiff's Federal constitutional rights that I have described to you;
2. That in so doing the defendant(s) acted "under color" of the authority of the State of _____; and
3. That the defendant's(s') acts were the legal cause of the plaintiff's damages.

[In this case the parties have stipulated (agreed) that the defendants acted "under color" of state law and you must accept that fact as proven]; or

[State or local officials act "under color" of the authority of the State when they act within the limits of their lawful authority. However, they also act "under color" of the authority of the State when they act without lawful authority or beyond the bounds of their lawful authority if their acts are done while the officials are purporting or pretending to act in the performance of their official duties. An official acts "under color" of state authority if he abuses or misuses a power that he possesses only because he is an official.]

[Include here the relevant instructions regarding liability of superior officers and the municipality, Sec. 10.3, post.]

The first aspect of the plaintiff's claim is that he was arrested and deprived of liberty "without due process of law." This means he was deprived of liberty

CIVIL RIGHTS   10.1

without authority of law. You must first decide whether the defendant(s) committed the acts that the plaintiff claims he (they) committed; and, if so, you must then decide whether the defendant(s) were acting within or beyond the bounds of their lawful authority under State law. If the defendant(s) acted within the limits of his (their) lawful authority under State law, then he (they) did not deprive the plaintiff of any right "without due process of law."

In that regard you are instructed that under the law of the State of _____

> [a police officer has the right to arrest a person without a warrant whenever the officer reasonably believes that such person has committed a misdemeanor offense in the presence of the officer. You are further instructed that, under the law of the state of _____ it is a misdemeanor offense for any person to be intoxicated and endanger the safety of another person or property.]

The second aspect of the claim is that the plaintiff was subjected to an unreasonable search of his home. The Constitution protects every citizen against "unreasonable" searches. Ordinarily, a law enforcement officer may not search a home before he has obtained a search warrant from a judicial officer. However, there are certain exceptions to this requirement. One is a search conducted by consent. If a person in lawful possession of a home freely and voluntarily invites or consents to a search, law enforcement officers may reasonably and lawfully conduct the search to the extent of the consent which the possessor gives. Another exception is an emergency situation. A law enforcement officer who has a reasonable and good faith belief that there is a serious threat to his safety or the safety of someone else may enter and make a safety inspection of a dwelling for the purpose of insuring or protecting his well-being and the well-being of others.

10.1 PATTERN JURY INSTRUCTIONS

The third aspect of the plaintiff's claim is that the defendant(s) used excessive force in making the arrest. Every person has the constitutional right not to be subjected to unreasonable or excessive force while being arrested by law enforcement officers, even though such arrest is otherwise proper. However, in making a lawful arrest, an officer has the right to use such force as is necessary under the circumstances to complete the arrest. You must determine whether the force used in making the arrest of the plaintiff was unnecessary, unreasonable or excessively violent. The force used in making an arrest is unnecessary, unreasonable or excessively violent if the arresting officer exceeded that degree of force which a reasonable and prudent law enforcement officer would have applied in making the arrest under the same circumstances.

The plaintiff must also prove by a preponderance of the evidence that the act or failure to act by the defendant was a cause-in-fact of the damage plaintiff suffered. An act or a failure to act is a cause-in-fact of an injury or damages if it appears from the evidence that the act or omission played a substantial part in bringing about or actually causing the injury or damages. The plaintiff must also prove by a preponderance of the evidence that the act or failure to act by the defendant was a proximate cause of the damage plaintiff suffered. An act or omission is a proximate cause of the plaintiff's injuries or damages if it appears from the evidence that the injury or damage was a reasonably foreseeable consequence of the act or omission.[1]

If you find that the plaintiff has proven his claim, you must then consider the defendant's(s') defense that

---

1. See Anderson v. Nosser, 456 F.2d 835 (5th Cir.1972), *affirmed sub nom.* Nosser v. Bradley, 409 U.S. 848, 93 S.Ct. 53, 34 L.Ed.2d 89 (1972); Reimer v. Smith, 663 F.2d 1316 (5th Cir.1981). See also S. Nahmod, Civil Rights and Civil Liberties Litigation—The Law of Section 1983, sections 3.17 and 3.18 (second edition 1986).

CIVIL RIGHTS 10.1

his (their) conduct was objectively reasonable in light of the legal rules clearly established at the time of the incident in issue and that the defendant(s) is (are) therefore not liable.

Police officers are presumed to know about the clearly established constitutional rights of citizens. (Here, announce the Court's ruling on what constitutional right involved was clearly established.)

If, after considering the scope of discretion and responsibility generally given to police officers in the performance of their duties, and after considering all of the surrounding circumstances of the case as they would have reasonably appeared at the time of the arrest, you find from a preponderance of the evidence that plaintiff has proved either (1) that the defendant(s) was (were) plainly incompetent or that (2) he (they) knowingly violated the law regarding the plaintiff's constitutional rights, you must find for the plaintiff. If, however, you find that the defendant(s) had a reasonable belief that his (their) actions did not violate the constitutional rights of the plaintiff, then you cannot find him (them) liable even if the plaintiff's rights were in fact violated as a result of the defendant's(s') objectively reasonable action.[2]

[Include here the relevant instructions from the Damages section, infra, with enumeration of the recoverable elements of damage and an explanation, as appropriate, of the terms used in describing each element.]

---

2. In Mangieri v. Clifton, 29 F.3d 1012 (5th Cir.1994) the Fifth Circuit instructs that the question of the objective reasonableness of the officer's conduct, the second part of the two-part inquiry for qualified immunity, is for the Court to decide, not the jury. Therefore, in instances in which the underlying historical facts about what occurred are not in dispute, the issue of the availability of the qualified immunity defense must be resolved at the summary judgment stage by the Court, not in a trial by the jury. Compare Presley v. City of Benbrook, 4 F.3d 405, 409, 410 n. 5 (5th Cir.1993).

10.2

ALTERNATIVE EXCESSIVE FORCE SECTION 1983 JURY CHARGE

The plaintiff in this action claims that the defendant violated plaintiff's constitutional rights when he used excessive and unnecessary force in arresting the plaintiff. As a result of the defendant's actions, the plaintiff claims that he suffered injury for which he seeks damages.

The defendant denies that any of his actions during the time in question violated the plaintiff's constitutional rights. The defendant claims that he was acting in good faith and with probable cause. The defendant further claims that he was not guilty of any fault or wrongdoing in regard to the incident sued upon.

Section 1983 of Title 42 of the United States Code provides that any citizen may seek redress in this court by way of damages against any person who, under color of state law or custom, intentionally deprives that citizen of any rights, privileges, or immunities secured or protected by the constitution or laws of the United States.

In order to prove his claim under this statute, the plaintiff must establish by a preponderance of the evidence each of the following elements:

(1) the defendant intentionally committed acts which operated to deprive the plaintiff of a right secured by the Constitution of the United States;

(2) the defendant acted under color of the authority of the State of _____;

(3) that the defendant's acts were the legal cause of the plaintiff's damages.

In this case you are instructed that the defendant was acting under color of state law at the time of the

CIVIL RIGHTS   10.2

acts complained of. The plaintiff alleges that the defendant used excessive force in arresting her.

United States citizens are protected against the use of excessive force by the Fourth Amendment to the Constitution. In order to prove that the defendant used excessive force in violation of the Fourth Amendment, the plaintiff must prove by a preponderance of the evidence:

1. some harm, that
2. resulted directly and only from the use of force that was clearly excessive to the need; and the excessiveness of which was
3. objectively unreasonable in light of the facts and circumstances at the time.

If the plaintiff fails to prove any one of these elements, you must find for the defendant.

Some of the things you may want to consider in determining whether the defendant(s) used excessive force are (1) the extent of the injury suffered, (2) the need for the application of force, (3) the relationship between the need and the amount of force used, (4) the threat reasonably perceived by the responsible officials, and (5) any efforts made to temper the severity of a forceful response. Injuries which result from, for example, an officer's use of force to overcome resistance to arrest do not involve constitutionally protected interests. An officer's use of excessive force does not give constitutional protection against injuries that would have occurred absent the excessive force.

The reasonableness of a particular use of force must be judged from the perspective of a reasonable officer on the scene, rather than with the 20/20 vision of hindsight. The nature of reasonableness must embody allowance for the fact that police officers are often forced to make split-second judgments—in circumstances that are tense, uncertain, and rapidly evolving—about the

10.2 PATTERN JURY INSTRUCTIONS

amount of force that is necessary in a particular situation.

This reasonableness inquiry is an objective one: the question is whether the officer's actions are objectively reasonable in light of the facts and circumstances confronting them, without regard to their underlying intent or motivation.

If you find that the plaintiff has proven his claim, you must then consider the defendant's(s') defense that his (their) conduct was objectively reasonable in light of the legal rules clearly established at the time of the incident in issue and that the defendant(s) is (are) therefore not liable.

Police officers are presumed to know about the clearly established constitutional rights of citizens. (Here, announce the Court's ruling on what constitutional right involved was clearly established.)

If, after considering the scope of discretion and responsibility generally given to police officers in the performance of their duties, and after considering all of the surrounding circumstances of the case as they would have reasonably appeared at the time of the arrest, you find from a preponderance of the evidence that plaintiff has proved either (1) that the defendant(s) was (were) plainly incompetent or that (2) he (they) knowingly violated the law regarding the plaintiff's constitutional rights, you must find for the plaintiff. If, however, you find that the defendant(s) had a reasonable belief that his (their) actions did not violate the constitutional rights of the plaintiff, then you cannot find him (them) liable even if the plaintiff's rights were in fact violated as a result of the defendant's(s') objectively reasonable action.[1]

---

1. In Mangieri v. Clifton, 29 F.3d 1012 (5th Cir.1994) the Fifth Circuit instructs that the question of the objective reasonableness of the officer's conduct, the second part of the two-part inquiry for qualified immunity, is for the Court to decide, not the jury. Therefore, in instances in which the

CIVIL RIGHTS 10.2

The plaintiff must also prove by a preponderance of the evidence that the act or failure to act by the defendant was a cause-in-fact of the damage the plaintiff suffered. An act or a failure to act is a cause-in-fact of an injury or damages if it appears from the evidence that the act or omission played a substantial part in bringing about or actually causing the injury or damages. The plaintiff must also prove by a preponderance of the evidence that the act or failure to act by the defendant was a proximate cause of the damage plaintiff suffered. An act or omission is a proximate cause of the plaintiff's injuries or damages if it appears from the evidence that the injury or damage was a reasonably foreseeable consequence of the act or omission.[2]

If you should find for the plaintiff and against the defendant, then you must decide the issue of damages.

---

underlying historical facts about what occurred are not in dispute, the issue of the availability of the qualified immunity defense must be resolved at the summary judgment stage by the Court, not in a trial by the jury. Compare Presley v. City of Benbrook, 4 F.3d 405, 409, 410 n. 5 (5th Cir.1993).

2. Johnson v. Morel, 876 F.2d 477, 479 (5th Cir.1989). See Anderson v. Nosser, 456 F.2d 835 (5th Cir.1972), affirmed sub nom. Nosser v. Bradley, 409 U.S. 848, 93 S.Ct. 53, 34 L.Ed.2d 89 (1972); Reimer v. Smith, 663 F.2d 1316 (5th Cir.1981). See also S. Nahmod, Civil Rights and Civil Liberties Litigation—The Law of Section 1983, sections 3.17 and 3.18 (second edition 1986). In Knight v. Caldwell, 970 F.2d 1430 (5th Cir.1992) the court adapted the Hudson v. McMillian approach and held that a significant injury is no longer required in an excessive force claim by an arrestee. See Hudson v. McMillian, 503 U.S. 1, 112 S.Ct. 995, 117 L.Ed.2d 156, 60 U.S.L.W. 4151 (1992); Pattern Jury Instructions 10.5 infra.

10.3

CIVIL RIGHTS—42 USC SECTION 1983 (SUPERIOR OFFICERS AND MUNICIPALITIES)

In addition to his claims against [police officers/officials of the municipal department] whom the plaintiff claims violated his constitutional rights, the plaintiff is suing superior officials, in this case [chief of police] [municipality]. To recover against a superior official, the plaintiff must show that the [chief of police] [supervisor of municipal department] [mayor of the municipality] had a legal duty to act to prevent the misdeeds of [police officers/officials of municipal department] and the [chief of police] [municipality]'s failure to act amounted to gross negligence or deliberate indifference of plaintiff's rights.[1]

The plaintiff claims that the City of _____, a municipality, is liable for the alleged constitutional deprivations. A city is liable for the deprivation of a constitutional right if the deprivation was pursuant to governmental custom, policy, ordinance, regulation or decision. Therefore, if you find that the plaintiff was injured as the proximate or legal result of [name of municipality]'s policy, custom, ordinance, regulation or decision, whether made by its lawmakers or by those officials whose edicts or acts may fairly be said to represent official policy, the city itself will be responsible.

The [mayor/city council] is an official whose acts constitute final official policy of the City of _____. Therefore, if you find that the acts of the [mayor/city council] deprived the plaintiff of constitutional rights, the City of _____ is liable for such deprivations.

1. Auster Oil & Gas, Inc. v. Stream, 835 F.2d 597, 602 (5th Cir.1988) *cert. denied,* Carmouche v. Auster Oil & Gas, Inc., 488 U.S. 848, 109 S.Ct. 129, 102 L.Ed.2d 102 (1988). *See also,* S. Nahmod, Civil Rights and Civil Liberties Litigation—The Law of Section 1983 § 3.16 (2nd ed. 1986).

10.4

CIVIL RIGHTS—42 USC SECTION 1983 (ADVERSE EMPLOYMENT DECISION—EXERCISE OF FIRST AMENDMENT RIGHTS)

[The plaintiff claims that the defendant(s), while acting "under color of state law," intentionally deprived the plaintiff of rights under the Constitution of the United States.]

The plaintiff claims that while the defendant(s) were acting under color of authority of the State of _____ [as members of the _____ School Board] he (they) intentionally violated the plaintiff's constitutional rights. The plaintiff claims that when the defendant(s) [discharged the plaintiff from employment] [failed to promote the plaintiff] because of the plaintiff's exercise of the right of free speech, the defendant(s) deprived him of his rights under the First Amendment of the Constitution.

The First Amendment of the Constitution of the United States gives every citizen the right to freedom of speech, which includes [describe the relevant free speech activity in which plaintiff allegedly engaged.]

A person may sue for an award of money damages against anyone who, "under color" of any State law or custom, intentionally violates the plaintiff's rights under the Constitution of the United States.

Thus, the plaintiff must prove by a preponderance of the evidence each of the following:

1. That the actions of the defendant(s) were "under color" of the authority of the State of _____;

2. That the plaintiff's speech activities were Constitutionally "protected" under the First Amendment;

3. That the plaintiff's exercise of protected First Amendment rights was a substantial or motivating factor in the defendant(s) decision [to discharge the plaintiff from employment/not to promote the plaintiff];

4. That the defendant(s') acts were the proximate or legal cause of the plaintiff's damages.

[In this case the Parties have stipulated (agreed) that the defendant(s) acted "under color" of state law. You must accept that fact as proven.]

or

[State or local officials act "under color" of the authority of the State when they act within the limits of their lawful authority. However, they also act "under color" of the authority of the State when they act without lawful authority or beyond the bounds of their lawful authority if their acts are done while the officials are purporting or pretending to act in the performance of their official duties. An official acts "under color" of the state authority if he abuses or misuses a power that he possesses only because he is an official.]

[Include here the relevant instructions regarding liability of superior officers and the municipality.]

In determining whether the defendant(s) intentionally violated the plaintiff's First Amendment rights, you must remember that the plaintiff as a public employee has a right to practice freedom of speech only to the extent that it does not unduly interfere with the duties and responsibilities of the plaintiff's employment. In determining whether the plaintiff's speech activities in this case were protected activities under the First Amendment, you must balance the plaintiff's First Amendment interests against the defendant(s') interests in promoting the efficiency of the public service it performs through its employees. Therefore, if you find under all the circumstances presented that a reasonable public employer could not have concluded that the plaintiff's speech activities unduly interfered with the duties and responsibilities of the plaintiff's employment, you must find that the speech was protected First Amendment expression.

To prove that his speech activities were a substantial or motivating factor in the defendant's(s') decision, the plaintiff does not have to prove that those speech activities were the only reason the defendants made the decision. The plaintiff need only prove that the speech activities were a substantial consideration that made a difference in or influenced the defendant's(s') decision.

The plaintiff must also prove by a preponderance of the evidence that the act or failure to act by the defendant was a cause-in-fact of the damage plaintiff suffered. An act or a failure to act is a cause-in-fact of an injury or damages if it appears from the evidence that the act or omission played a substantial part in bringing about or actually causing the injury or damages. The plaintiff must also prove by a preponderance of the evidence that the act or failure to act by the defendant was a proximate cause of the damage plaintiff suffered. An act or omission is a proximate cause of the plaintiff's injuries or damages if it appears from the evidence that the injury or damage was a reasonably foreseeable consequence of the act or omission.[1]

[If you find that the plaintiff has established each element of his claim, you must then decide whether the defendant(s) have shown by a preponderance of the evidence that he (they) would [have dismissed] [not have promoted] the plaintiff for other reasons even if plaintiff had not exercised his protected speech activity. If you find that the defendant(s) would [have dismissed]

---

1. See Anderson v. Nosser, 456 F.2d 835 (5th Cir.1972), *affirmed sub nom.* Nosser v. Bradley, 409 U.S. 848, 93 S.Ct. 53, 34 L.Ed.2d 89 (1972); Reimer v. Smith, 663 F.2d 1316 (5th Cir.1981). See also S. Nahmod, Civil Rights and Civil Liberties Litigation—The Law of Section 1983, sections 3.17 and 3.18 (second edition 1986).

10.4 PATTERN JURY INSTRUCTIONS

[not have promoted] the plaintiff for reasons apart from the speech activity, then your verdict should be for the defendant(s).]

If you find for the plaintiff and against the defendant(s) on their defense, you must then decide the issue of the plaintiff's damages.

[Include here the relevant instructions from the Damages section, infra, with enumeration of the recoverable elements of damage and an explanation, as appropriate, of the terms used in describing each element.]

10.5

EIGHTH AMENDMENT (EXCESSIVE FORCE)

Plaintiff claims that the defendant, by using excessive and unnecessary force against him, violated plaintiff's Eighth Amendment constitutional rights.

Inmates are protected from cruel and unusual punishment under the Eighth Amendment of the United States Constitution. In order to prove a violation under the Eighth Amendment, the plaintiff must show that the defendant(s) unnecessarily and wantonly inflicted pain on him. Whether a use of force against a prison inmate is unnecessary or wanton depends on whether force was applied in a good faith effort to maintain or restore discipline, or whether it was done maliciously or sadistically to cause harm. In order to prove a violation under the Eighth Amendment in this case, therefore, the plaintiff must prove each of the following two elements by a preponderance of the evidence:

First: That the defendant(s) used force against the plaintiff maliciously and sadistically, for the very purpose of causing plaintiff harm; and

Second: That plaintiff suffered some harm as a result of the defendant's use of force.

If the plaintiff fails to prove either of these elements, you must find for the defendant. The first element is to be evaluated by a subjective analysis of the defendant(s) and his state of mind at the time. To act "maliciously" means to intentionally do a wrongful act without just cause or excuse, with an intent to inflict injury or under circumstances that show an evil intent. In deciding whether this element has been proved, I remind you that you must give prison officials wide ranging deference in the adoption and execution of policies and practices that in their judgment are needed to preserve internal order and discipline and to maintain internal security in the prison.[1]

Some of the things you may want to consider in determining whether the prison officials unnecessarily and wantonly inflicted pain on the plaintiff include (1) the extent of the injury suffered, (2) the need for the application of force, (3) the relationship between the need and the amount of force used, (4) the threat reasonably perceived by the responsible officials, and (5) any efforts made to temper the severity of a forceful response.

---

1. See Hudson v. McMillian, 503 U.S. 1, 112 S.Ct. 995, 117 L.Ed.2d 156, 60 U.S.L.W. 4151 (1992). In *Hudson,* the Supreme Court overruled well-settled Fifth Circuit precedent which held that a prison inmate claiming that his Eighth Amendment rights were violated by a use of excessive force had to show that he suffered "serious" injury. *Hudson* held that the "core judicial inquiry" in all prison *excessive force cases* under the Eighth Amendment is "whether force was applied in a good-faith effort to maintain or restore discipline, or maliciously and sadistically to cause harm." Id., 503 U.S. at 1, 112 S.Ct. at 996, 60 U.S.L.W. at 4153. This inquiry is not objective, but, rather, delves into the state of mind of the prison official. Further, the Court's holding seems to be that this is the extent of the analysis when excessive force is alleged in a prisoner case.

The Court held that the "objective" component of the Eighth Amendment analysis, tied to "contemporary standards of decency," is always satisfied, regardless of how badly the prisoner was hurt, when a prison official maliciously and sadistically inflicts harm on an inmate. Id.

The objective analysis is now more significant in Eighth Amendment cases when prisoners allege that they received inadequate medical care or were subject to unconstitutional conditions of confinement. In such cases inmates still must establish objectively that they were subject to a "serious" deprivation. *Id.*

On remand, the Fifth Circuit in *Hudson* enumerated the five factors listed as being among the several factors that are relevant to the test for unnecessary and wanton infliction of pain in the Eighth Amendment context. Hudson v. McMillian, 962 F.2d 522 (5th Cir.1992).

10.6

EIGHTH AMENDMENT (INADEQUATE MEDICAL CARE)

Plaintiff claims that prison officials, by demonstrating deliberate indifference to his serious medical needs, violated his Eighth Amendment constitutional rights.

Inmates are protected from cruel and unusual punishment under the Eighth Amendment of the United States Constitution. In order to prove a violation under the Eighth Amendment, the plaintiff must show that the defendant(s) unnecessarily and wantonly inflicted harm on him.

To show that his Eighth Amendment rights were violated because he received inadequate medical care, the plaintiff must prove that defendant(s) exhibited deliberate indifference to his serious medical needs. In order to prove a violation under the Eighth Amendment in this case, therefore, the plaintiff must prove each of the following three elements by a preponderance of the evidence:

First: That defendant(s) displayed deliberate indifference to an illness or injury of the plaintiff;

Second: That the plaintiff's illness or injury was serious; and

Third: That the plaintiff was injured as a result of the prison officials acts or omissions regarding his illness or injury.

If the plaintiff fails to prove any of these elements, you must find for the defendant(s). The first element is to be evaluated by a subjective analysis of the defendant(s) and his state of mind. To act "deliberately" means to act intentionally; that is, knowingly and voluntarily and not because of mistake or accident.

10.6 PATTERN JURY INSTRUCTIONS

The second element is to be examined objectively, focusing on the specific illness or injury and the reasonably foreseeable consequences to the plaintiff of a deprivation of care or inadequate care.[1] That is, would a reasonable person acting under the same circumstances foresee that the conduct of the defendant(s) would cause the harm plaintiff claims?

---

1. See Hudson v. McMillian, 503 U.S. 1, 112 S.Ct. 995, 117 L.Ed.2d 156, 60 U.S.L.W. 4151 (1992); Estelle v. Gamble, 429 U.S. 97, 97 S.Ct. 285, 50 L.Ed.2d 251 (1976).

10.7

EIGHTH AMENDMENT
(CONDITIONS OF CONFINEMENT)

Plaintiff claims that the conditions of his confinement in _____ (prison) (jail) were such that they violated his Eighth Amendment constitutional rights.

Inmates are protected from cruel and unusual punishment under the Eighth Amendment of the United States Constitution. In order to prove a violation under the Eighth Amendment, the plaintiff must show that he was unnecessarily and wantonly caused pain.

To show that his Eighth Amendment rights were violated because of the conditions of his confinement, the inmate must prove by a preponderance of the evidence that the prison conditions resulted in a serious deprivation of his basic human needs. It is not enough that the conditions were restrictive or even harsh; this is part of the penalty that criminal offenders must pay. Rather, you may find that the conditions of the plaintiff's confinement were cruel and unusual only if they deprived him of the minimal civilized measure of life's necessities. The test is an objective one, and in applying it, you should be guided by society's contemporary standards of decency.[1] What you must decide, then, is whether, under the circumstances, the conditions of confinement about which the plaintiff complains were reasonable or not.

---

1. See Hudson v. McMillian, 503 U.S. 1, 112 S.Ct. 995, 117 L.Ed.2d 156, 60 U.S.L.W. 4151 (1992); Rhodes v. Chapman, 452 U.S. 337, 101 S.Ct. 2392, 69 L.Ed.2d 59 (1981).

11. LABOR AND EMPLOYMENT CLAIMS

WESTLAW Electronic Research
See WESTLAW Electronic Research Guide preceding the Table of Contents.

11.1

FAIR LABOR STANDARDS ACT (29 U.S.C. SEC. 216)

This case arises under the Fair Labor Standards Act, a federal law that provides for the payment of minimum wages [and/or time-and-a-half overtime pay]. The plaintiff claims that the defendant did not pay him the legally required minimum wage [and/or overtime pay].

The plaintiff must prove each of the following by a preponderance of the evidence:

1. That the defendant employed the plaintiff during the time period involved;
2. That [the plaintiff's work was engaged in commerce or in the production of goods for commerce] [the defendant's business or businesses under unified operation or common control employed at least two persons and was engaged in commerce or the production of goods for commerce and had annual gross sales of at least $500,000];[1] and
3. That the defendant failed to pay the plaintiff the minimum wage [and/or overtime pay] required by law.

---

1. *See* The Federal Labor Standards Act of 1989; *see also* 29 U.S.C. §§ 203(s), 206; West's Federal Practice Manual § 1451.6 and Supplement 1451.6.

11.1 PATTERN JURY INSTRUCTIONS

The term "commerce" has a very broad meaning and includes any trade, commerce, transportation, transmission or communication between any state and any place outside that state.

A person is considered to have been "engaged in the production of goods" if the person produced, manufactured, mined, handled, transported, or in any other manner worked on such goods or worked in any closely related process or occupation directly essential to the production of the goods.

The minimum wage during the period of time involved in this case was $_____ per hour.

In determining whether an employer has paid the minimum wage, the employer is entitled to a credit for the reasonable costs it incurred in furnishing certain items such as meals, lodging, or other facilities if the employer regularly provided the meals, lodging, or other facilities for the benefit of the employee.

An employer must pay its employees at least one and one-half times their regular rate for overtime work.

An employee's regular rate is the basis for calculating any overtime pay due the employee.

The regular rate for a week is determined by dividing the first 40 hours worked into the total wages paid for those 40 hours. The overtime rate, then, is one and one-half times that rate.

In its defense, the defendant claims that even if you should find that the plaintiff has proved all the necessary elements of his/her claim, the minimum wage law [the overtime pay law] does not apply because the defendant is exempt from those requirements.

The exemption claimed by the defendant is [*insert applicable exemption*].

To receive the benefit of this exemption, the defendant must prove by a preponderance of the evidence [*list or describe essential elements of the claimed exemption*].

LABOR AND EMPLOYMENT CLAIMS   11.1

If, after considering all of the evidence, you find that the plaintiff has failed to prove one or more of the elements of his (her) claim, your verdict must be for the defendant.

Even if the plaintiff has proven the elements of his (her) claim, you must return a verdict for the defendant if the defendant proves by a preponderance of the evidence that it is exempt from the minimum wage law [overtime pay law].

If, however, you find that the plaintiff has proved by a preponderance of the evidence all of the elements of his claim, and that the defendant has failed to establish its claim of exemption from the minimum wage law [or, the overtime pay law], then your verdict must be for the plaintiff and you must determine the damages that the plaintiff is entitled to recover.

The measure of damages is the difference between what the employer should have paid the employee under the law and the amount that you find the employer actually paid.

11.2

AGE DISCRIMINATION IN EMPLOYMENT ACT (29 U.S.C. SECTIONS 621–634)

The plaintiff claims that the defendant discriminated against the plaintiff by discharging him and later failing to rehire him because of his age.

Specifically, the plaintiff claims that [*describe the specific act asserted as discrimination on the part of the defendant*].

The defendant denies that [*describe the specific act and defendant's defenses, if any*].

It is unlawful for an employer to discharge [discriminate against] an employee between the ages of forty and seventy because of that employee's age.

The plaintiff must prove by a preponderance of the evidence each of the following:

1. That he was between the ages of forty (40) and seventy (70);
2. That he was discharged [discriminated against], and
3. That his age was one of the reasons the defendant discharged [discriminated against] him. He need not prove that age was the only reason.

If you find that the plaintiff has established each of these elements of his claim, you must then consider the defendant's defenses. The defendant makes this (these) defense(s):

[That age is a good faith occupational qualification] [and] [that the treatment of the plaintiff was in accordance with the terms of a good faith seniority system.]

The law permits an employer to discharge an employee when the discharge is based upon that (either of those) ground(s). Thus if you find that the defendant

LABOR AND EMPLOYMENT CLAIMS 11.2

has established, by a preponderance of the evidence, [that age is a bona fide occupational qualification] [that the treatment of the plaintiff was in accordance with the terms of a good faith seniority system] you must find for the defendant.

[To establish a "good faith occupational qualification," an employer must prove that he has reasonable cause to believe that all or substantially all of a class of applicants would be unable to perform a job safely and efficiently, and that the occupational qualification is "reasonably necessary to the essence" of the business operation.]

[To qualify as a "good faith seniority system" the system must use the length of service as a primary criteria for the fair allocation of available employment opportunities among younger and older workers.]

[To summarize, the plaintiff must prove by a preponderance of the evidence that the defendant discriminated against him because of his age.]

[However, should the defendant seek to justify the termination of the plaintiff on the basis of an occupational qualification, or seniority system, then the defendant must prove by a preponderance of the evidence that the defendant did in fact terminate the plaintiff's employment on the basis of an occupational qualification or seniority system as defined in this instruction.]

If you find that the defendant discriminated against the plaintiff, then you must determine the amount of damages the plaintiff has suffered.

[*Enumerate recoverable elements of damage with explanation, as appropriate, of the terms used in describing each element.*]

11.3

EMPLOYEE'S CLAIM AGAINST EMPLOYER AND UNION

The plaintiff makes two claims. The plaintiff first claims that his employer discharged him without just cause in violation of the collective bargaining agreement that governs the terms and conditions of the plaintiff's employment. The plaintiff's second claim is that the union breached its duty to fairly represent him as one of its members. Specifically, the plaintiff claims that the union failed to investigate [or otherwise process] the plaintiff's grievance against his employer under the grievance procedure provided by the collective bargaining agreement.

[As to the first claim, you are instructed that an employer may only discharge an employee governed by a collective bargaining agreement if there is just cause for the employee's dismissal. Just cause means a real cause or basis for dismissal and not an arbitrary whim. A just cause is a cause that a reasonable employer, acting in good faith in similar circumstances, would regard as a good and sufficient basis for terminating the services of an employee.]

To win on his first claim, the plaintiff must prove both of the following by a preponderance of the evidence:

1. That his employer discharged him from his employment, and

2. That the discharge was without just cause.

If you find for the plaintiff on the first claim, you must then consider the second claim.

A union has a duty under the law to fairly represent the interests of its members in protecting their rights under a collective bargaining agreement. As to the plaintiff's second claim, the plaintiff must prove by a preponderance of the evidence that the union breached its duty to fairly represent the plaintiff's interests under the collective bargaining agreement.

However, an individual employee does not have an absolute right to require his union to pursue a grievance against his employer. A union has considerable discretion in controlling the grievance and arbitration procedure. The question is not whether the employee is satisfied with the union representation or whether that representation was perfect.

The test is basic fairness. So long as the union acts in good faith, it may exercise its discretion in determining whether to pursue or process an employee's grievance against the employer. Even if an employee's grievance has merit, the union's mere negligence or its exercise of poor judgment does not constitute a breach of its duty of fair representation. But where a union acts in bad faith and with hostility, discrimination or arbitrariness fails to process a meritorious grievance, the union violates its duty to fairly represent the union member who has made the grievance.

DAMAGES

The amount of your verdict should be a sum that you find fairly compensates the plaintiff for the damages he has incurred. The measure of damages to which the plaintiff is entitled, if any, is the amount which the plaintiff would have earned from his employment with the employer if he had not been discharged. You must reduce this amount by any earnings that the plaintiff earned, or reasonably could have earned, from other employment. [The plaintiff has the duty to mitigate or minimize his damage. The defendants are not responsible for lost earnings that the plaintiff could have avoided if he had used reasonable care in seeking other employment to avoid or minimize the injury.]

11.3 PATTERN JURY INSTRUCTIONS

Once you have arrived at a figure for lost wages or damages, you must apportion those damages between the employer and the union. In making the apportionment, you should follow this guideline. The employer is liable for lost wages due solely to its breach of the collective bargaining agreement in discharging the plaintiff. The union is responsible for any increases in lost wages caused by its failure to process the plaintiff's grievance.

12. TAX REFUNDS

WESTLAW Electronic Research

See WESTLAW Electronic Research Guide preceding the Table of Contents.

In each of the following tax refund charges, the following introductory sentence may be appropriate:

In this case the plaintiff seeks a refund of taxes that he has paid.

12.1

REASONABLE COMPENSATION TO STOCKHOLDER—EMPLOYEE

The plaintiff is entitled to certain tax deductions that are ordinary and necessary business expenses, such as reasonable salaries or other compensation paid for personal services actually rendered.

However, a corporation is not entitled to a deduction for dividends it pays to its shareholders. Dividends paid by a corporation to its shareholders are a distribution of profits, not deductible expenses.

The Commissioner of Internal Revenue must disallow any portion of a compensation deduction that the Commissioner believes is (1) not compensation or (2) unreasonable in amount. This prevents a corporation from improperly reducing its taxes by distributing all or some of its profits to its shareholders and calling the distribution something else, like salaries.

You must decide whether the plaintiff may deduct on its federal income tax returns for the years involved certain amounts it says it paid as salaries. To be entitled to the salary deductions claims, the plaintiff

12.1   PATTERN JURY INSTRUCTIONS

must establish each of the following by a preponderance of the evidence:

1. that the payments were actually paid as compensation for services rendered and were not a distribution of the profits of the business, and
2. that the payments are reasonable when compared with the personal services actually rendered.

The fact that the plaintiff called the payments salary, compensation or bonus is not determinative.

Reasonable compensation is the amount that is paid for similar services, by similar enterprises, under similar circumstances to a qualified person, whether that person is a shareholder of the corporation or not.

In deciding what is reasonable compensation, you may consider all of the following factors:

1. The size, nature and complexity of the plaintiff's business.
2. The quality and quantity of the services actually rendered by the employee, including the difficulty or simplicity of the work and the responsibility assumed by the employee.
3. The qualifications, experience and background of the employee, including any special training and formal education.
4. Whether or not all of the employee's time was devoted to the business, or whether the employee devoted time to other businesses, interests and activities.
5. The salaries paid to others employed by the plaintiff and whether and how much stock they owned in the corporation.
6. What a comparable business pays for comparable services.

TAX REFUNDS 12.1

7. The relationship between the amounts paid to the employee and the employee's shareholdings in the plaintiff.

8. The dividend history of the plaintiff.

9. Whether the amount paid was set or adjusted after the profits for the year were known.

10. The extent of control which the employee or a member of the employee's family had over the corporation in setting the amount of the payment.

11. Whether the person or persons setting the amount of the payment did so with a view of avoiding payment of corporate taxes on that amount.

No one factor is controlling. You should make your decision after consideration of all the evidence.

[Remember that this case does not involve the plaintiff's right to pay any amount it wishes to any employee it chooses. The only issue is whether all of the amounts that were paid qualify as a tax deduction.]

12.2

DEBT vs. EQUITY

A corporation may deduct from its gross income for income tax purposes any amounts it pays as interest on money that it has borrowed. However, a corporation may not deduct from its taxable income any dividends it pays to its shareholders. [The fact that the amount paid is taxable to the recipient, either as interest or as a dividend, is irrelevant.]

Here, the Commissioner of Internal Revenue determined that the payments that the stockholders in it made to the plaintiff were investments by them in the capital of the corporation and not loans to the corporation, and that the later payments the plaintiff made to those stockholders were dividend distributions and were not interest payments on loans to the company. As a result, the Commissioner disallowed the deductions the plaintiff claimed for payments as interest. The plaintiff has the burden of proving that the Commissioner's determination was incorrect.

You must decide whether the stockholders' payments to the plaintiff created a good faith indebtedness—a true loan—or whether they were made as investments in the capital of the corporation. A person may be both an investor and a creditor in the same corporation but, as I shall explain later, status as one or the other is not necessarily determined by the label that the parties attached to the transaction.

An investment in capital is an advance made to a corporation by a stockholder as an investment for the purpose of making a profit. Whether the stockholder makes a profit is dependent upon and measured by the future success of the business. In other words, the stockholder making the advance intends to make an investment and take the risks associated with the venture. The corporation is not committed to repay the money to him. The stockholder-investor anticipates a return out of future profits of the enterprise. A return is by no means certain, however, since an investment in capital is similar to any other investment that is dependent upon future profits and earnings.

A "loan" is an advance of money pursuant to an agreement that the money will be repaid at some future date. The agreement and obligation to repay must be absolute. Of course, the lender takes the risk that the corporation may not be able to repay the loan; however, the obligation to do so continues to exist without regard to the financial ability of the corporation.

The essential difference between a stockholder who makes a capital investment and a creditor who loans money to the corporation is that the stockholder's intention is to embark upon the corporate venture as an owner with all associated risks of loss in order to reach his goal of making a profit. The creditor, however, does not intend to take such risks so far as they may be avoided, but merely lends money to others who intend to take the risk.

There is no single test to determine whether advances by stockholders to a corporation are considered as loans to the corporation or as capital investments in the corporation. You must consider all of the facts of this case and determine the true substance of the transaction. Neither names nor labels are determinative. The substance and not the form is controlling. You must examine the transaction in terms of what the parties intended to accomplish and what they actually accomplished; you should not be misled by the symbols, labels or forms they used.

In determining whether the transaction was a loan or an investment, you may consider the following factors:

1. The presence or absence of a maturity date. The presence of a fixed maturity date indicates a fixed

obligation to repay, a characteristic of a loan. The absence of a fixed maturity date indicates that repayment was in some way tied to the fortunes of the business, which is a characteristic of a stockholder's investment.

2. Whether there is an expectation of payment at maturity. If there is such an expectation, this is an indication of the existence of a debt. If there is no real expectation of payment at maturity or if there is an unreasonably postponed due date on the note representing the advance, this indicates that the advance was intended to be an investment.

3. Whether the corporation established a sinking fund (that is, a fund in which money is accumulated to pay a loan when it becomes due); whether the corporation had the notes of the stockholder subordinated to other indebtedness; whether the corporation prevailed upon its stockholders to postpone or forego payments of the amounts that they termed principal, or interest. Any of these acts would indicate that there was a reasonable expectation of payment at maturity. However, if the corporation did not establish a sinking fund, or did not have the stockholders to subordinate to other creditors, or postpone payment of the stockholder's notes, this may indicate that there was no good expectation of payment at maturity.

4. The source of the payments. If repayment is possible only out of corporate earnings, the transaction looks like a contribution of equity capital. If, however, repayment is not dependent upon earnings, the transaction looks like a loan to the corporation.

5. An increased participation in management. If the contributors were granted an increased voting power or participation in the affairs of the corporation by virtue of the advance, this indicates that the advance was an investment. If the contributors were not granted any increased voting power or participation in the

corporation's affairs by virtue of the advance, this would indicate that the transaction was a loan and not an investment in capital.

6. How the corporation treated other creditors. If the corporation paid other creditors upon the maturity of the corporation's obligations to them, but advances to the corporation by its stockholders were not so paid, this indicates that the advances by the stockholders were capital investments, and not true loans.

7. Whether there was "thin" or inadequate capitalization. Thin capitalization is evidence of a capital contribution where the debt to equity ratio was initially high. As to the debt to equity ratio, if the amount of the debt is much higher, or several times higher, than the amount of capital stock, this would tend to indicate that the advances in question were capital investments. If the amount of debt is more nearly equal to, or is less than, the amount of capital stock, this indicates that the advances represented true indebtedness.

8. If the corporation makes so called "interest" payments but does so only when profits are available, this indicates a capital investment; if regular payments are made, whether profits are available or not, this indicates that the transaction was a loan and not an investment in capital.

9. The identity of interests between creditor and stockholder. If stockholder advances are made in proportion to their respective stock ownership, it looks like an equity capital contribution. A sharply disproportionate ratio between a stockholder's percentage interest in stock and the debt strongly indicates that the debt is a true loan.

10. The corporation's ability to obtain loans from outside sources. If the corporation has the ability to borrow funds from outside sources at the time an advance by a shareholder is made, then the advance looks like a true loan. If no reasonable creditor would have

12.2 PATTERN JURY INSTRUCTIONS

loaned funds to the corporation at the time of the advance, an inference arises that a reasonable shareholder also would not do so, and the transaction has the appearance of an investment in capital.

No single factor or consideration is controlling; your decision should be made on the basis of all the evidence in the case.

12.3

EMPLOYEE vs. INDEPENDENT CONTRACTOR

The law requires every employer that pays wages to an employee to deduct and withhold a certain amount of taxes from the gross wages of the employee. The employer pays those taxes to the Federal Government for the employee.

If the employer fails to withhold the necessary taxes from the employee's wages, the employer is required to pay the amount that it should have withheld.

The plaintiff has made certain payments to the Federal Government as taxes deducted and withheld from employee's wages. The plaintiff contends that it was not liable for the amount it paid, and thus is entitled to a refund on the ground that _____ were not its employees, but were, instead, independent contractors. If they were not the plaintiff's employees, then the plaintiff is entitled to recover the money. If they were employees of the plaintiff, then the plaintiff is not entitled to recover the money it paid.

The sole issue for you to decide is whether, during the time in question, _____ were employees of the plaintiff or whether they were independent contractors.

There are a number of factors you must take into consideration in making that determination. No one factor is controlling. Your determination should be made from all of the evidence in this case.

One of the most important considerations is the degree of control the plaintiff exercised over the work of _____. An employer has the right to control an employee. Thus, it is important to determine whether the plaintiff had the right to direct and control _____ not only as to the results of _____'s work, but also as to the details, manner and means by which those results were accomplished. You must determine whether the plaintiff had the right to control the number and the frequency of breaks, how _____ performed their work, the type of equipment they could use, and their work schedule. If you find that the plaintiff had the right to supervise and control those details, and the manner and means by which the results were to be accomplished, this indicates that there was an employer-employee relationship between the plaintiff and _____. A finding that the plaintiff did not exercise such elements of supervision and control over _____ would support a finding that _____ were independent contractors and not the plaintiff's employees. It is the right to control and not the actual exercise of control that is important.

Another factor you should consider is whether _____ were (individually) carrying on an independent business or whether they regularly worked in the course of the plaintiff's business. For this purpose, you may consider whether _____ advertised or generally offered their services to others; whether or not they, as individuals or as a group, used a business name in dealing with the plaintiff; whether they listed themselves in any business capacity in city or telephone directories; whether they maintained their own offices; whether they procured necessary licenses for the carrying on of their activities; whether they supplied their own tools or equipment; and any other evidence tending to show that they were carrying on an independent business as individuals or as a group.

Another factor you should consider is the term and duration of the relationship between the plaintiff and _____. The relationship of an independent contractor generally contemplates the completion of an agreed service within a stipulated period of time. An employment relationship generally involves a continuous rendering of services for an indefinite period of time.

Another factor you may consider is the manner of payment. An independent contractor generally is one who has the opportunity to make a profit, or the risk of taking a loss; an employee generally does not have the opportunity to make a profit, or the risk of loss. An employee generally is paid on a time or piecework or commission basis, while an independent contractor is ordinarily paid an agreed amount—or according to an agreed formula basis—for a given job.

The description the parties give to their relationship is not controlling. You must determine whether the relationship between the plaintiff and the _____ is one of employment or of independent contract, taking into account all of the factors I have mentioned to you and all of the evidence in this case.

12.4

BUSINESS LOSS vs. HOBBY LOSS

The controversy in this case concerns the deductibility of expenses involved in the operation of _____. The plaintiff contends that he operated _____ as a business for profit, and therefore is entitled to a deduction from income tax for the years _____ for the losses he sustained in operating _____. The Government contends that plaintiff operated _____ for personal pleasure, enjoyment and prestige, that the plaintiff did not have a profit motive in operating _____ and that, as a consequence, the plaintiff is not entitled to deduct the losses that resulted from operating _____.

A taxpayer is allowed to deduct all of the ordinary and necessary expenses paid or incurred in carrying on a trade or business. Moreover, if a taxpayer sustained a loss during a particular year, he may deduct that loss from income derived from other sources, such as the plaintiff has done here. The key words are "trade or business." If expenses or losses occur in a trade or business, they are deductible. If a person is engaged in an activity simply for pleasure or recreation or social prestige and not to make a profit, the expenses incurred in the activity are not deductible. An activity is a trade or business only when a taxpayer enters into the activity with the real expectation of making a profit.

To constitute a business, the activity usually must be carried on regularly and continuously, over a period of time. Generally, a person engaged in a business activity holds himself out as selling goods or services, and regularly devotes time and attention to that activity. However, the activity need not be the taxpayer's only occupation or even his principal occupation. It may be a sideline, so long as it occupies the time, attention and labor of the taxpayer for the purpose of profit, not as a mere recreation or hobby. In this regard, you may consider the plaintiff's regular occupation and the amount of income derived from that occupation. You may also compare the character of his regular occupation with the size and character of the activity in question in this case and the time he expended on each.

If you find that the plaintiff had a profit motive, then the fact that the plaintiff's activities were conducted in the face of serious losses, standing alone, does not necessarily mean that those activities were for the plaintiff's personal pleasure.

If the taxpayer sincerely and in good faith hopes and expects to make a profit from the activity, then the fact that others may believe that there was no reasonable expectation of profit from the activity does not prevent it from being a business.

In determining whether the plaintiff intended to engage in the activity for profit, no one factor is controlling. After considering all of the evidence, you must decide whether the plaintiff has proved by a preponderance of the evidence that the activity in question constituted the conduct of a trade or business, or whether the plaintiff engaged in such activity as a hobby or for recreation or other similar purposes and not for profit. [You must determine separately for each of the years involved whether the activity in question was a trade or business conducted for profit. It may be a business one year and not the next, or vice versa. However, in determining whether the activity was a business in a particular year, you may consider the fact that the activity was or was not a business in a year prior or subsequent to the particular year you are considering.]

12.5

REAL ESTATE HELD PRIMARILY FOR SALE

The plaintiff claims he is entitled to treat the gain from the sale of the properties in question as capital gain, subject to the lower capital gain tax rate. The Government contends that the gain should be taxed at the higher ordinary income tax rates.

You must decide whether or not the plaintiff is entitled to treat the gain from the sale of the properties in question as capital gain.

A gain qualifies for capital gain tax treatment if the plaintiff proves by a preponderance of the evidence, first, the plaintiff held each of the parcels of property for more than six months prior to sale; and second, the plaintiff did not hold the properties primarily for sale to customers in the ordinary course of a trade or business.

[The parties agree that the properties in question were held by the plaintiff for more than six months prior to the sale.]

[You must determine whether the plaintiff held the properties in question for more than six months prior to the sale. If he did not, then you must find that the plaintiff is not entitled to treat the gain as capital gain.]

[If he did, then] [Thus] you must decide whether, at the time of the sale, the plaintiff was holding the properties in question primarily for sale to customers in the ordinary course of the plaintiff's trade or business. "Primarily" means "of first importance" or "principally."

In making your decision you must carefully scrutinize the circumstances surrounding the plaintiff's ownership and sale of these properties. While the reason the plaintiff acquired the property is entitled to some weight, the ultimate question is the reason why the plaintiff held the property at the time of sale. Property that was originally acquired for investment may change in character to property held for sale to customers in the ordinary course of a trade or business. If the plaintiff held the property for investment in the hope that it would appreciate in value without any further activity on the plaintiff's part, this would indicate that the property was a capital asset. However, if the plaintiff held the property in the hope that it could be developed and then resold in the ordinary course of the plaintiff's trade or business, this would be evidence that it was held primarily for sale. You may consider the following factors in making your decision:

1. The extent to which the plaintiff (or others acting on the plaintiff's behalf) engaged in developing or improving the properties. If there was development or improvement, this would indicate that the plaintiff was holding the properties for sale to customers in the ordinary course of his trade or business.

2. The number, continuity and frequency of the sales. The presence of extensive and continuous sales activity over a period of time would indicate that the plaintiff held the properties in question for sale to customers in the ordinary course of a trade or business. Limited sales on an infrequent basis are evidence that the plaintiff did not hold the properties for sale to customers in the ordinary course of a trade or business.

3. The solicitation of customers. If the plaintiff (or others acting on the plaintiff's behalf) actively solicited customers, this would indicate that the plaintiff was holding the properties in the ordinary course of a trade or business. If the plaintiff advertised the properties for sale, this would be evidence that he was holding the properties for sale to customers in the ordinary

course of trade or business. However, if the plaintiff did not actively solicit customers and did not advertise the properties for sale, it is evidence that the properties were not held for sale to customers in the ordinary course of a trade or business.

4. The income the plaintiff derived from the sale of the properties in relation to income from other sources. If a substantial part of the plaintiff's income was derived from the sales of these properties, this is an indication that the sales activity constituted the conduct of a trade or business. If the income derived was not substantial in relation to income from other sources, this is an indication that the sale of the properties did not constitute a trade or business.

5. The holding period of the property. The shorter the elapsed time between the plaintiff's acquisition of the properties and the disposition of them, the more reasonable it is to conclude that plaintiff held the properties for sale to customers in the ordinary course of a trade or business. Conversely, the longer the holding period, the more it appears that the plaintiff held the properties for investment purposes.

These are not exclusive factors. They are guidelines. There may be other factors that you may consider that I have not mentioned, and you should bear in mind that no one factor is determinative of the issue before you. In making your decision you should carefully weigh all of the evidence.

12.6

SECTION 6672 PENALTY

_____, a corporation, withheld from the wages and salaries of its employees federal income taxes and social security taxes totaling $_____. The corporation failed to pay to the Government the amount withheld, as it was required to do under the law, and it then became insolvent and had no funds from which the Government could collect the withheld taxes.

The law provides that a person associated with a corporation who has the duty and responsibility to see that the taxes are paid to the Government, and who willfully fails to do so, is personally liable to the Government in the form of a penalty for the amount of taxes withheld but not paid. This generally is referred to as the 100 percent penalty because the amount of the penalty is equal to the amount of taxes that were withheld but not paid. Thus, the penalty is merely a means of collecting the taxes withheld and not paid in order to make the Government whole.

The employer, a corporation, can act only through its officers, directors and employees. Every corporation that is an employer must have some person or persons, but at least one, who has the duty or responsibility of withholding and paying the taxes which the law requires the corporation to withhold and to pay to the Government. More than one person may be liable for the 100 percent penalty.

The Government contends that the plaintiff was one of the persons responsible for collecting and paying to it the taxes that were withheld. The Government also contends that the failure of the plaintiff to pay over those taxes was willful. The plaintiff has the burden of proving to you, by a preponderance of the evidence, either that the plaintiff was not a person whose duty it was to collect and pay to the Government the taxes in question, or that the plaintiff did not willfully fail to collect and pay over such taxes.

Thus the first issue is whether the plaintiff was a responsible person. The term responsible person includes any person who is connected or associated with the corporation-employer in such a manner that he has the power to see that the taxes are paid, or the power to make final decisions concerning the corporation, or the power to determine which of the corporation's creditors are to be paid and when they are to be paid. The term responsible person may include corporate officers, employees, members of the board of directors or stockholders. The meaning of the term responsible person is broad and is not limited to the person who actually prepares the payroll checks or the tax returns. One may be a responsible person although he is not authorized to draw checks for the corporation, so long as he has the power to decide who will receive the corporate funds. In other words, the responsible person is any person who can effectively control the finances of the corporation, or determine which of the corporation's bills should or should not be paid.

If you conclude that the plaintiff was not a responsible person, then you need not consider any other issue, and you must find in favor of the plaintiff. However, if you find that the plaintiff was a responsible person, you then must decide whether the plaintiff acted willfully in the failure to pay the withheld taxes to the Government.

The term willfully means that the act of failing to pay over the taxes was voluntarily, consciously and intentionally done without reasonable cause. If the responsible person consciously, voluntarily and intentionally used, or caused to be used, the funds that were withheld to pay taxes for some other purpose, then he has acted willfully. It is not necessary to find that the plaintiff had bad motives. It must only be shown that the plaintiff made the deliberate choice to use the funds

TAX REFUNDS 12.6

in some way other than to pay the Government. If you find that, at a time when withheld taxes were due and owing to the Government, the plaintiff used corporate funds to pay suppliers, or employees' net take home salaries, or rent, or any creditor, including the plaintiff, or in any way other than paying the Government the withheld wages of the employees as their federal income taxes and social security taxes, you must find that the plaintiff acted willfully in failing to see that the withheld taxes were paid. It is no excuse or defense that the responsible person, in good faith, hoped to pay the taxes at a later time, or relied upon the advice and information furnished by accountants and attorneys.

12.7

GIFTS IN CONTEMPLATION OF DEATH

Any gift made by a person within the three years immediately before his death is presumed to have been made in contemplation of death. Unless the plaintiff establishes by a preponderance of the evidence that the gift by _____ was not made in contemplation of death, the fair market value of that gift must be included in _____'s gross estate for federal estate tax purposes.

The Commissioner of Internal Revenue determined in this case that the gifts were made in contemplation of death, and therefore assessed additional taxes against the estate. The plaintiff challenges the Commissioner's determination.

The term "in contemplation of death" does not have reference to a general expectation of death that all of us share. On the other hand, its meaning is not restricted to a fear or belief that death is imminent or near. Rather, a transfer is "in contemplation of death" if it is prompted by the thought of death (although the thought of death may not be the only thing that prompts it). A transfer is prompted by the thought of death if it is made either with the purpose of avoiding death taxes, or if it is made for any other motive associated with death.

Thus the issue is _____'s state of mind when the transfer of the property was made. Stated another way, you must determine what prompted _____ at the time of the transfer, to make the transfer. You must determine his motives by considering all of the facts and circumstances surrounding the transfer.

In this connection, you should consider the following questions:

1. What was _____'s age at the time of the transfer? A transfer made by a person in advanced

years is more likely to be in contemplation of death than a transfer made by a person who is not advanced in years.

2. What was the cause of _____'s death? A transfer made by a person who is in bad health and who knows of the bad health is more likely to be in contemplation of death than a transfer made by a person who is in good health and who knows of the good health.

3. What was the relative value of the property given away? If the value of the property transferred by _____ is small in comparison to the overall value of his (her) estate, this is an indication that the transfer was not made in contemplation of death. However, if the property transferred had a substantial value and comprised a substantial portion of _____'s estate prior to the transfer, this may be an indication that the transfer was made in contemplation of death.

4. Who was the recipient or donee of the gift? A transfer to a person who would normally have received the property upon the transferor's death is more likely to be in contemplation of death than a transfer to a person who would not normally have received the property upon the transferor's death.

5. Had _____ made such gifts before? If a person had a history of making gifts, this indicates that the transfer involved was not made in contemplation of death. If _____ did not have a history of making gifts, the fact that he (she) began making gifts shortly before death is an indication that they were made in contemplation of death.

6. Were the gifts made pursuant to a specific plan? If you find that _____ made this transfer pursuant to a plan to reduce the amount of the taxes that would be due on his (her) estate, then it is more likely that the transfer was made in contemplation of death. On the other hand, a finding that the transfer was not made in order to reduce taxes does not necessarily mean that it

12.7 PATTERN JURY INSTRUCTIONS

was not made in contemplation of death, since it may still have been a substitute for giving property by will at death.

Each of these factors is relevant in assisting you to reach your determination, but no single factor is controlling. If you find that the plaintiff has proved by a preponderance of the evidence that a life motive was the dominant motive that prompted _____ to make the gifts, then the plaintiff has overcome the presumption that the gifts were made in contemplation of death and you should find for the plaintiff. If you find that a death motive was the dominant motive that prompted _____ to make the gifts, then you must find for the Government.

After considering all of the facts and circumstances, you may find that the decedent had mixed motives for making these gifts and that those motives associated with life were evenly balanced by other motives associated with death. If you do, you must find for the Government, because the plaintiff has failed to prove to you by a preponderance of the evidence that the transfer was not made in contemplation of death.

13. MISCELLANEOUS FEDERAL CLAIMS

WESTLAW Electronic Research
See WESTLAW Electronic Research Guide preceding the Table of Contents.

13.1

AUTOMOBILE DEALERS DAY–IN–COURT ACT (15 U.S.C. SECTION 1221)

The plaintiff claims that the defendant failed to act in good faith in [terminating] [cancelling] [not renewing] the plaintiff's written franchise agreement.

[Each party to an automobile franchise agreement (and all officers, employees or agents of each party) must act in good faith. They must act in a fair and equitable manner toward each other. Each party must be free from coercion, intimidation or threats of coercion or intimidation from the other party.]

The plaintiff must prove each of the following by a preponderance of the evidence:

1. That the defendant failed to act in good faith in the [termination] [cancellation] [nonrenewal] of the franchise;
2. That the defendant's conduct amounted to coercion or intimidation, or threats toward the plaintiff; and
3. That the plaintiff suffered damages as a result of the defendant's conduct.

The fact that a dealer has a written franchise agreement with a manufacturer does not give the dealer the right to have the written agreement renewed when it expires. However, the manufacturer must act in good faith in determining whether to renew the agreement. The manufacturer is not prohibited from enforcing reasonable provisions of the contract or from advancing its own business interests by making recommendations [urgings] [arguments] that will encourage the dealer to engage in more efficient operations or to sell more.

The issue is not whether the defendant acted unfairly or inequitably in its business relations with the plaintiff; the issue is only whether the defendant failed to act in good faith and whether its actions toward the plaintiff amounted to coercion and intimidation.

To prove coercion or intimidation, the plaintiff must prove by a preponderance of the evidence there was conduct on the part of the defendant that resulted in the plaintiff's acting [refraining from acting] against its will. The plaintiff must show that it was coerced in some way into doing something it had a lawful right not to do, or into not doing something it had a lawful right to do. The coercion or intimidation must include a wrongful demand by the defendant that would result in penalties or sanctions if not complied with.

The coercion or intimidation must be actual; the mere fact that a dealer believes that it has been coerced or intimidated is not sufficient.

DAMAGES

If you find in favor of the plaintiff, you must then consider the issue of the plaintiff's damages. You should award the plaintiff an amount of money that will fairly compensate it for the damage the evidence shows it has sustained and is reasonably certain to sustain in the future as a result of the failure to renew the franchise.

[Enumerate recoverable elements of damages, as appropriate, in light of the evidence.]

13.2

ODOMETER REQUIREMENTS, MOTOR VEHICLE INFORMATION AND COST SAVINGS ACT (15 U.S.C. SECTION 1981)

The plaintiff claims that the defendant violated a federal law against tampering with odometers on motor vehicles.

An odometer is a vehicle's mileage indicator, the instrument that measures and records the total, actual distance a motor vehicle has traveled.

The plaintiff claims that the defendant, with the intent to defraud, changed the odometer to show a lower number of miles than the vehicle actually had traveled [*modify to reflect specifically charged conduct proscribed by the act*].

The plaintiff must prove by a preponderance of the evidence both:

1. That the defendant [or its agents] changed the number of miles indicated on the odometer, and

2. He (they) made the change with the intent to defraud someone.

The plaintiff must prove that the defendant intended to defraud someone. However, it is not necessary that the plaintiff prove that the defendant intended to defraud the plaintiff, or that the defendant actually defrauded the plaintiff or anyone else.

A person acts with intent to defraud when he acts with the specific intent to deceive or cheat, ordinarily for the purpose of achieving some financial gain for himself.

The plaintiff must prove that the defendant knew, or should have known, of the discrepancy in mileage.[1]

---

1. Nieto v. Pence, 578 F.2d 640 (5th Cir.1978).

13.2 PATTERN JURY INSTRUCTIONS

If the plaintiff establishes his claim by the preponderance of the evidence, then you must determine the amount of actual damages he suffered. In this case, actual damages means (1) the difference between the price the plaintiff paid for the vehicle and the fair market value of the vehicle, with its actual mileage, at the date of the sale to the plaintiff, and (2) any other damages the plaintiff may have suffered as a result of the purchase.

[*Note that attorneys' fees are also recoverable. 15 U.S.C. Sec. 1989.*]

13.3

EMINENT DOMAIN

This suit is brought by the United States in the exercise of its power of eminent domain and is called a condemnation proceeding.

The Government has the right and the power to take private property for public purposes. That power is essential to the Government's independence. If the Government did not have the power to take private property, any landowner could delay or even prevent public improvements, or could force the Government to pay a price that exceeds the fair market value of the property taken.

However, exercise of the power of eminent domain is subject to the requirement that the United States must pay fair market value to the owner for all property taken.

Fair market value means the amount a willing buyer would have paid a willing seller in an arms-length transaction, when both parties are fully informed about all of the advantages and disadvantages of the property, and neither is acting under any compulsion to buy or sell.

Fair market value must be determined at the time of the taking, considering the property's highest and most profitable use, in the open market with a reasonable time allowed to find a purchaser.

The burden is on the owner to prove, by a preponderance of the evidence, the fair market value of his property at the date of the taking.

The highest and most profitable use of property is the use for which it was actually and potentially suitable and adaptable. It is not necessarily the use the owner was making of the property at the time of taking.

Sometimes the fact that the Government plans to take property will cause an increase or decrease in the property's fair market value at the time of the taking. In determining fair market value, you should not consider the fact that the Government had plans to take the land. Instead, you should fix the fair market value on the date of the taking without regard to any threat or possibility of a taking.

[Where the property that is taken constitutes only a part of an owner's interest, the owner is entitled to both the value of the interest actually taken, and to an additional amount equal to the decrease, if any, of the fair market value of the owner's interest in the land that was not taken.]

[The Government contends that the portion of defendant's land that was not taken in this proceeding increased in value because of the public improvements which the Government made after taking the property. Two types of benefits may result from a public improvement: general benefits and special benefits. General benefits are those that result not only to property of the defendant landowner, but also to the property in the community generally. Special benefits are those that accrue specially to a particular piece of land and not to all property in the community generally.] [You may not consider any increase in value because of general benefits, but you must consider any increase due to special benefits.]

[The judgment I will enter upon your verdict will provide that the Government pay interest to compensate the landowner for any delay in payment caused by the Government, after the date of taking. Therefore, you should not consider any delay in payment and you should not include any interest, or other compensation for the delay, in your verdict.]

13.4

INTERSTATE LAND SALES FULL DISCLOSURE ACT (15 U.S.C. SECTION 1709)

The plaintiff, _____ claims that the defendant, _____ violated the Interstate Land Sales Full Disclosure Act. Under that law, a real estate developer is prohibited from using [the mails or] any [other] means of communication in interstate commerce for the sale [lease] of lots in a subdivision unless the developer has furnished the purchaser with a document called a property report before the signing of any contract for sale [lease].

[The property report should inform a buyer about all material facts so that the buyer may make an informed decision whether to enter into an agreement with the seller. The property report must specify (*describe the type of information germane to plaintiff's claims and information required to be included in a property report under Section 1707*).]

[The plaintiff claims that the defendant (made an untrue statement of a material fact) (omitted a material fact which was required to be stated) in the property report. The plaintiff claims the defendant (*describe the statement or omission*).]

To establish his claim, the plaintiff must prove the following three elements by a preponderance of the evidence:

1. That the property report [contained an untrue statement] [omitted a fact required to be stated];
2. That the [untrue statement] [omitted fact] was material; and
3. That the plaintiff suffered damages.

If the property report contained a [misstatement] [omission], the plaintiff does not need to prove that the defendant intended to make it or that he even knew of it. The plaintiff is only required to prove that the defendant made the [misstatement] [omission].

A [misstatement] [omission] is material if a reasonable investor would have considered it to be important in making the decision to [buy] [lease] the property.

If you find that the plaintiff has established his claim, you must then consider the plaintiff's damages. To determine the amount of damages you may take into account the contract price of the [lot] [leasehold]; the amount plaintiff actually paid; the reasonable cost of any improvements; the fair market value of the [lot] [leasehold] at the time the plaintiff brought this suit; and the fair market value of the [lot] [leasehold] when the plaintiff [purchased] [leased] it. In addition, your award of damages may include interest, court costs, independent appraisers' fees, and travel to and from the premises and reasonable amounts for attorneys' fees. However, you may award only those damages established by a preponderance of the evidence as necessary to fairly compensate the plaintiff; the law does not allow you to make an award of damages for the purpose of punishing the defendant.

14. MISCELLANEOUS FEDERAL DEFENSES

WESTLAW Electronic Research
See WESTLAW Electronic Research Guide preceding the Table of Contents.

14.1

STATUTE OF LIMITATIONS DEFENSE

The defendant asserts as a defense that the statute of limitations bars the plaintiff's claim. A statute of limitations is a law that provides that a suit is barred if a plaintiff does not bring it within a prescribed period of time. The time period within which the suit must be brought begins when the plaintiff first knew, or by the exercise of reasonable care, should have known that

[*describe the operative fact triggering the statute of limitations*].

The applicable statute of limitations period is ___ years, and the defendant claims that the plaintiff's suit is barred here because the plaintiff knew, or by the exercise of reasonable care should have known, more than ___ years before bringing this suit that

[*describe the operative fact triggering the statute of limitations*].

The defendant has the burden of proving the statute of limitations defense. In other words, he must prove by a preponderance of the evidence that plaintiff did not bring the suit within the applicable time period.

*

15. DAMAGES

WESTLAW Electronic Research

See WESTLAW Electronic Research Guide preceding the Table of Contents.

15.1

CONSIDER DAMAGES ONLY IF NECESSARY

If the plaintiff has proven his claim against the defendant by a preponderance of the evidence, you must determine the damages to which the plaintiff is entitled. You should not interpret the fact that I have given instructions about the plaintiff's damages as an indication in any way that I believe that the plaintiff should, or should not, win this case. It is your task first to decide whether the defendant is liable. I am instructing you on damages only so that you will have guidance in the event you decide that the defendant is liable and that the plaintiff is entitled to recover money from the defendant.

15.2

COMPENSATORY DAMAGES

If you find that the defendant is liable to the plaintiff, then you must determine an amount that is fair compensation for all of the plaintiff's damages. These damages are called compensatory damages. The purpose of compensatory damages is to make the plaintiff whole—that is, to compensate the plaintiff for the damage that the plaintiff has suffered. [Compensatory damages are not limited to expenses that the plaintiff may have incurred because of his injury. If the plaintiff wins, he is entitled to compensatory damages for the physical injury, pain and suffering, mental anguish, shock and discomfort that he has suffered because of the defendant's conduct.]

You may award compensatory damages only for injuries that the plaintiff proves were proximately caused by the defendant's allegedly wrongful conduct. The damages that you award must be fair compensation for all of the plaintiff's damages, no more and no less. [Damages are not allowed as a punishment and cannot be imposed or increased to penalize the defendant.] You should not award compensatory damages for speculative injuries, but only for those injuries which the plaintiff has actually suffered or that the plaintiff is reasonably likely to suffer in the future.

If you decide to award compensatory damages, you should be guided by dispassionate common sense. Computing damages may be difficult, but you must not let that difficulty lead you to engage in arbitrary guesswork. On the other hand, the law does not require that the plaintiff prove the amount of his losses with mathematical precision, but only with as much definiteness and accuracy as the circumstances permit.

You must use sound discretion in fixing an award of damages, drawing reasonable inferences where you find

DAMAGES 15.2

them appropriate from the facts and circumstances in evidence.

You should consider the following elements of damage, to the extent you find them proved by a preponderance of the evidence:

[Select appropriate charges from Section 15.3, et seq.][1]

---

1. It should be noted that Section 104(a) of the Internal Revenue Code was recently amended to provide that an award of both compensatory or punitive damages received on account of a purely non-physical injury would be fully subject to income tax. Although the amendment does not apply to claims for physical injury, however, the United States Supreme Court has held that all punitive damages are subject to income tax because they are not awarded "on account of personal injuries or sickness." Thus, it would seem as though any award of punitive damages would be subject to income tax, and that an award of compensatory damages for non-physical injuries would be subject to income tax. A cautionary instruction should be given in the case of all punitive damages, and in the case of awards for compensatory damages based on non-physical injuries. (See O'Gilvie, et al. v. United States, ___ U.S. ___, 117 S.Ct. 452, 136 L.Ed.2d 454 (1996).)

15.3

CALCULATION OF PAST AND FUTURE DAMAGES

A. Damages Accrued

If you find for the plaintiff, he is entitled to recover an amount that will fairly compensate him for any damages he has suffered to date.

B. Calculation of Future Damages

If you find that the plaintiff is reasonably certain to suffer damages in the future from his injuries, then you should award him the amount you believe would fairly compensate him for such future damages. [In calculating future damages, you should consider the standard table of mortality as compiled by the United States Bureau of the Census, or other recognized mortality table.]

C. Reduction of Future Damages to Present Value

An award of future damages necessarily requires that payment be made now for a loss that plaintiff will not actually suffer until some future date. If you should find that the plaintiff is entitled to future damages, including future earnings, then you must determine the present worth in dollars of such future damages.

If you award damages for loss of future earnings, you must consider two particular factors:

1. You should reduce any award by the amount of the expenses that the plaintiff would have incurred in making those earnings.

2. If you make an award for future loss of earnings, you must reduce it to present value by considering the interest that the plaintiff could earn on the amount of the award if he made a relatively risk-free investment. The reason why you must make this reduction is because an award of an

DAMAGES 15.3

amount representing future loss of earnings is more valuable to the plaintiff if he receives it today than if he received it in the future, when he would otherwise have earned it. It is more valuable because the plaintiff can earn interest on it for the period of time between the date of the award and the date he would have earned the money. Thus you should adjust the amount of any award for future loss of earnings by the amount of interest that the plaintiff can earn on that amount in the future.

If you make any award for future medical expenses, you should adjust or discount the award to present value in the same manner as with loss of future earnings.

However, you must not make any adjustment to present value for any damages you may award for future pain and suffering or future mental anguish.

15.4

INJURY/PAIN/DISABILITY/DISFIGUREMENT/LOSS OF CAPACITY FOR ENJOYMENT OF LIFE

You may award damages for any bodily injury that the plaintiff sustained and any pain and suffering, [disability], [disfigurement], [mental anguish], [and/or] [loss of capacity for enjoyment of life] that the plaintiff experienced in the past [or will experience in the future] as a result of the bodily injury. No evidence of the value of intangible things, such as mental or physical pain and suffering, has been or need be introduced. You are not trying to determine value, but an amount that will fairly compensate the plaintiff for the damages he has suffered. There is no exact standard for fixing the compensation to be awarded for these elements of damage. Any award that you make should be fair in the light of the evidence.

15.5

AGGRAVATION OR ACTIVATION OF DISEASE OR DEFECT

You may award damages for aggravation of an existing disease or physical defect [or activation of any such latent condition] resulting from physical injury to the plaintiff. If you find that there was such an aggravation, you should determine, if you can, what portion of the plaintiff's condition resulted from the aggravation, and make allowance in your verdict only for the aggravation.

15.6

MEDICAL EXPENSES

A. For Major Plaintiff

The reasonable [value] [expense] of [hospitalization and] medical [and nursing] care and treatment that the plaintiff will require because of his injuries which were caused by the defendant's wrongful conduct.

B. For Plaintiff's Minor Child

The reasonable [value] [expense] of [hospitalization and] medical [and nursing] care and treatment that the plaintiff [reasonably obtained for his child in the past] [will obtain for his child in the future] until the child reaches the age of majority.

C. For Minor Plaintiff (After Majority)

The reasonable [value] [expense] of [hospitalization and] medical [and nursing] care and treatment that the minor plaintiff reasonably will require after he reaches the age of majority.

15.7

LOST EARNINGS/TIME/EARNING CAPACITY

[Any earnings lost] [Any working time lost] [Any loss of ability to earn money sustained] in the past [and any such loss in the future].

15.8

SPOUSE'S LOSS OF CONSORTIUM AND SERVICES

Any past [and future] loss of his spouse's services, comfort, society and attention that the plaintiff has suffered [and will suffer] because of his spouse's injury.

15.9

PARENT'S LOSS OF CHILD'S SERVICES, EARNINGS, EARNING CAPACITY

Any loss of his child's services and earnings [or earning capacity] that the plaintiff has sustained in the past [and will sustain in the future, until the child reaches the age of majority] because of his child's injury.

15.10

PROPERTY DAMAGE

Any damage to the plaintiff's personal property. The measure of that damage is the difference between the fair market value of the property immediately before [the incident complained of] and the fair market value immediately after [the incident].

[If market value is not applicable] You may award as damages an amount equal to the cost of restoring the property to its condition prior to [the incident complained of]. [You also may take into consideration any loss the plaintiff sustained by being deprived of the use of the property during the period required for its [repair] [replacement].]

15.11

WRONGFUL DEATH—ESTATE DAMAGES

1. Lost Earnings

The estate's loss of earnings of the decedent from the date of injury to the date of death, less any amount you award for a survivor's loss of monetary support during that period.

2. Lost Accumulations

The estate's loss of net accumulations, that is, that part of the decedent's net income from [salary] [business] after taxes, including pension benefits [but excluding income from investments continuing beyond death] that the decedent, after paying personal expenses and monies for the support of the decedent's survivors, would have remaining as part of the estate if the decedent had lived his normal life expectancy.[1]

3. Medical or Funeral Expenses

Medical or funeral expenses resulting from the decedent's injury or death that [have become a charge against the decedent's estate] [were paid by or on behalf of the decedent by one other than a survivor].

---

1. The appropriateness of this charge depends upon the applicable substantive law. See, e.g., Miles v. Apex Marine Corp., 498 U.S. 19, 111 S.Ct. 317, 112 L.Ed.2d 275 (1990).

15.12

WRONGFUL DEATH—SURVIVORS' DAMAGES

1. Lost Support and Services

The loss of _____'s support and services that the plaintiff _____ has sustained [and will sustain in the future] because of _____'s death. You must determine the duration of any future loss by considering the joint life expectancy of _____ and the plaintiff _____. Joint life expectancy means the number of years that both _____ and _____ could have been expected to be alive together, considering the ages and life expectancy of each at the time of _____'s death. [Joint life expectancy means the number of years that the decedent could have expected to be alive during which the plaintiff would have been a minor child.]

In evaluating past and future loss of support and services, you must consider the plaintiff _____'s relationship to _____, the amount of _____'s probable net income available for distribution to the plaintiff _____ and the replacement value of _____'s services to the plaintiff _____. ["Support" includes contributions in kind as well as sums of money. "Services" means tasks that _____ regularly performed that now will be a necessary expense to the plaintiff _____ because of _____'s death.]

2. Medical and Funeral Expenses

[Medical] [and/or] [funeral] expenses due to _____'s injury or death paid by the plaintiff _____.

3. Surviving Spouse

The Plaintiff _____'s loss of companionship and protection, and his (her) mental pain and suffering that resulted from _____'s death. In determining the duration of these losses, you must consider the joint life expectancy of the decedent and the plaintiff _____.

DAMAGES 15.12

4. Surviving Minor Child

The loss of parental companionship, instruction, and guidance, and the mental pain and suffering [name all minor children] sustained because of _____'s death. In determining the duration of these losses, you must consider the joint life expectancy of the decedent and [the surviving child] [each of the surviving children].

5. Surviving Parent of Minor Child

The plaintiff _____'s mental pain and suffering resulting from the death of [his] [her] [their] minor child. In determining the duration of this mental pain and suffering, you must consider the life [expectancy] [expectancies] of the plaintiff and the minor child.

15.13

PUNITIVE DAMAGES

If you find that the defendant is liable for the plaintiff's injuries, you must award the plaintiff the compensatory damages that he has proven. You also may award punitive damages, if the plaintiff has proved that the defendant acted with malice or willfulness or with callous and reckless indifference to the safety or rights of others. One acts willfully or with reckless indifference to the rights of others when he acts in disregard of a high and excessive degree of danger about which he knows or which would be apparent to a reasonable person in his condition.

If you determine that the defendant's conduct was so shocking and offensive as to justify an award of punitive damages, you may exercise your discretion to award those damages. In making any award of punitive damages, you should consider that the purpose of punitive damages is to punish a defendant for shocking conduct, and to deter the defendant and others from engaging in similar conduct in the future. The law does not require you to award punitive damages, however, if you decide to award punitive damages, you must use sound reason in setting the amount of the damages. The amount of an award of punitive damages must not reflect bias, prejudice, or sympathy toward any party. However, the amount can be as large as you believe necessary to fulfill the purposes of punitive damages. You may consider the financial resources of the defendant in fixing the amount of punitive damages [and you may impose punitive damages against one or more of the defendants, and not others, or against more than one defendant in different amounts].[1]

1. On the general subject of punitive damages and the guidelines to be considered in fashioning jury charges, see Pacific Mutual Life Insurance Company v. Haslip, 499 U.S. 1, 111 S.Ct. 1032, 113 L.Ed.2d 1 (1991).

DAMAGES   15.13

It should be noted that Section 104(a) of the Internal Revenue Code was recently amended to provide that an award of both compensatory or punitive damages received on account of a purely non-physical injury would be fully subject to income tax. Although the amendment does not apply to claims for physical injury, however, the United States Supreme Court has held that all punitive damages are subject to income tax because they are not awarded "on account of personal injuries or sickness." Thus, it would seem as though any award of punitive damages would be subject to income tax, and that an award of compensatory damages for non-physical injuries would be subject to income tax. A cautionary instruction should be given in the case of all punitive damages, and in the case of awards for compensatory damages based on non-physical injuries. (See O'Gilvie, et al. v. United States, ___ U.S. ___, 117 S.Ct. 452, 136 L.Ed.2d 454 (1996).)

15.14

MULTIPLE CLAIMS—
MULTIPLE DEFENDANTS

You must not award compensatory damages more than once for the same injury. For example, if the plaintiff prevails on two claims and establishes a dollar amount for his injuries, you must not award him any additional compensatory damages on each claim. The plaintiff is only entitled to be made whole once, and may not recover more than he has lost. Of course, if different injuries are attributed to the separate claims, then you must compensate the plaintiff fully for all of his injuries.

With respect to punitive damages, you may make separate awards on each claim that plaintiff has established.

You may impose damages on a claim solely upon the defendant or defendants that you find are liable on that claim. Although there are [number] defendants in this case, it does not necessarily follow that if one is liable, all or any of the others also are liable. Each defendant is entitled to fair, separate and individual consideration of his case without regard to your decision as to the other defendants. If you find that only one defendant is responsible for a particular injury, then you must award damages for that injury only against that defendant.

You may find that more than one defendant is liable for a particular injury. If so, the plaintiff is not required to establish how much of the injury was caused by each particular defendant whom you find liable. Thus, if you conclude that the defendants you find liable acted jointly, then you may treat them jointly for purposes of calculating damages. If you decide that [two or more] [both] of the defendants are jointly liable on a particular claim, then you may simply determine the

DAMAGES 15.14

overall amount of damages for which they are liable, without determining individual percentages of liability.[1]

[1]. The instruction assumes that the court or jury has already determined that damages are not divisible and that all defendants are potentially jointly and severally (solidarily) liable. Likewise, in many cases it will, in fact, be necessary for the jury to apportion fault. For instance, such apportionment would be necessary if one defendant were seeking contribution from another or if the relevant substantive law no longer provided for unlimited joint and several liability. See, e.g., LSA–C.C. art. 2324. In such a case the court should instruct the jury that it must apportion fault between the various parties and the total allocated fault *must* add up to 100%.

15.15

MITIGATION OF DAMAGES

A person who claims damages resulting from the wrongful act of another has a duty under the law to use reasonable diligence to mitigate—to avoid or minimize those damages.

If you find the defendant is liable and the plaintiff has suffered damages, the plaintiff may not recover for any item of damage which he could have avoided through reasonable effort. If you find by a preponderance of the evidence the plaintiff unreasonably failed to take advantage of an opportunity to lessen his damages, you should deny him recovery for those damages which he would have avoided had he taken advantage of the opportunity.

You are the sole judge of whether the plaintiff acted reasonably in avoiding or minimizing his damages. An injured plaintiff may not sit idly by when presented with an opportunity to reduce his damages. However, he is not required to exercise unreasonable efforts or incur unreasonable expenses in mitigating the damages. The defendant has the burden of proving the damages which the plaintiff could have mitigated. In deciding whether to reduce the plaintiff's damages because of his failure to mitigate, you must weigh all the evidence in light of the particular circumstances of the case, using sound discretion in deciding whether the defendant has satisfied his burden of proving that the plaintiff's conduct was not reasonable.

†